HOW TO USE THIS BOO

Essentially this is a reference gu
and examples of the key terms
Programming).

Newcomers to NLP often find the key concepts and terms used to
be a barrier. The language is often technical and dense. My aim
is to provide the beginner with a set of accessible and everyday
definitions of this language, along with specific and simple
examples. I have also included stories which put the key terms
into context.

I have developed and tested this guide over several years, through
my teaching of Practitioner and Master Practitioner programmes.
My learners have told me they find this guide invaluable, and I
hope you do too.

The Guide is structured alphabetically. For each term, there is:
- **a definition of the term, in everyday language**
- one or more examples of the term in context
- further discussion of how and why the term is helpful
- *often an appropriate story*

If in any of the descriptions I use a word referred to elsewhere in
the Glossary, I will mark it using this <u>underlined font</u>. Though I have
consulted other texts extensively, I take full responsibility for all the
definitions and examples used.

For simplicity of writing style, I have referred throughout to the
person who is consciously using NLP as 'coach'. All names have
been changed to protect confidentiality.

Finally, I would like to thank all my learners, who over the years
have provided their own definitions and examples, which have
significantly contributed to this guide. This guide is dedicated to
them, and to all those who have shared the learning journey with
me. Thank you!

Arnie Skelton
March 2014

ALIGNMENT

See <u>ecology</u>.

Extent to which any chosen action is acceptable to, or in synch with, the rest of the individual's values, needs or drivers.

> taking more ownership does not put the individual under undue pressure or harm valued relationships

> committing to extra study does not conflict with having enough time for family life

This is the 'E' of PURE, itself used to explain the four requirements of a <u>Well Formed Outcome</u>.

For a solution to work for someone, that solution has to 'fit in' with all other aspects important to that individual. The phrase <u>NLP</u> uses to describe this 'compatibility' is 'ecologically sound': so any solution has to be 'ecologically sound', in terms of not being in conflict with any other aspect important to that individual.

Chris had lots of ability, and was committed to learning – but still struggled to learn. It was only when he switched his learning approach to something that worked for him (rather than worked for the school) that he began to make rapid progress. In NLP terms, the approach the school wanted Chris to take was not ecologically sound for Chris...

ALTERED STATE

A change in the individual's internal mentality and/or emotions, or external behaviour. A change in their thoughts, or thought patterns, or their feelings, or the way they act. Usually the change in the individual's external state is triggered by a change in their internal state (see also calibration).

This is a powerful concept within NLP. I like to explain it using the TEBI Model (© Effective Ltd):

Trigger → Emotion → Behaviour → Impact

A trigger (often an external threat, but sometimes an internal memory) creates an internal emotion, which creates a response in the individual's behaviour, leading to an impact or consequence, for the individual or others. The emotion and behaviour elements together represent the 'altered state'.

You will probably recognise and identify with this sequence, and will have many examples of it occurring, with varying degrees of impact. A key part of NLP is to help anyone for whom the TEBI sequence is problematic, and affecting their life in an unhelpful way. The aim, quite simply, is to help that individual create and maintain an altered state, from unhelpful to helpful. (See also state management and trance).

Once a new altered state has been achieved, it may then be useful to internalise it, to embed it as a new, permanent, state (see also strategy installation).

3

AMBIGUITY

Lack of certainty or clarity, due to the way in which words, symbols, and behaviours (including body language) are used.

In NLP, the focus is primarily on the way words are used (ie the 'linguistic' part of NLP) – see the four examples given below.

Often the ambiguity is accidental, but it can also be used deliberately. Ambiguity is the essence of a lot of humour. For example, Tommy Cooper, the legendary comedian, was (in)famous for his love of puns. For example:

"two aerials met on a roof and got married. The wedding was terrible but the reception was fantastic"

"two peanuts walked into a bar – unfortunately one was assaulted"

Both jokes – and many more like them – rely on the double meaning of key words or phrases. Ambiguity can be very helpful in activating the mind. In order to 'see' the ambiguity, different neurological connections have to be open: to 'get' the joke, the person has to be able to understand both meanings. If you like puns, you are likely to have a more 'open' mind....

So deliberately using ambiguity can reach different parts of the brain, and create 'hidden' messages: this can be particularly powerful if the conscious part of the brain makes one sense of the meaning, and the subconscious part of the brain hears and remembers a different but important meaning.

For example, look again at the paragraph above beginning 'Both jokes...': the phrase that follows - " – and many more like them – "

was probably interpreted by you as "and there are lots of other similar jokes".....but it could also mean "and many more people than me enjoy them". A general principle of NLP is that the subconscious is a powerful part of our mind, and often drives our everyday behaviour. So getting messages into someone's subconscious can be very important and powerful.

A key function of all ambiguities, whether intended or not, is to open up the mind, and create different/alternative thought patterns. In that sense, ambiguity invites curiosity. They are a form of indirect communication, and the deliberate use of ambiguity often regarded as a technique associated with the Milton Model.

One of the most famous murder trials in Britain focused on the ambiguous use of the words 'let him have it'. Bentley, the accused, was with his accomplice, and both were being chased by the police. Bentley's accomplice was carrying a gun, and, as the police closed in, Bentley told his accomplice to 'let him have it'. His accomplice shot the policeman, who died instantly. In the subsequent trial, Bentley insisted he meant 'give up the gun', and that his accomplice had mistakenly interpreted this as 'shoot him'. The jury believed the latter interpretation, and both men were hanged.

I was in hospital recently, and thought about the use of the word 'invalid'....and, on another occasion, down the corridor of a local authority leisure services department I noticed a sign on a door saying "complex staff"....

a

AMBIGUITY: PHONOLOGICAL

Two or more words that sound the same but have different meanings.

> here, hear
> no, know
> wait, weight

The words may even be spelled the same, but have different meanings...

> Are you following me?

Could mean – "do you understand what I'm saying?" – or it <u>could</u> mean "are you prepared to be led by me?"

I was on holiday recently, on the Greek island of Rhodes. I was hiring a car, and asked about 'the roads'. I got a description of the island, and places to visit. It was only later I realised that the person hiring the car had thought I had asked about Rhodes, the island.....

AMBIGUITY: PUNCTUATION

Creating two phrases joined by a phonological word.

> Glad to see you all here what I'm saying
> Do you want to follow the 'heard it before' brigade?

This looks clumsy on paper (<u>visual</u>) but can be very effective when spoken (<u>auditory</u>).

AMBIGUITY: SCOPE

Where it is unclear whether the descriptive word applies to the word it precedes only, or everything that follows.

> Red table and chair
> Great golf and tennis player

So in the above examples, is it only the table that is red, or also the chair? Is the person only a great golfer, or also a great tennis player?

This type of ambiguity could be used intentionally to create a particular, usually positive, impression. For example, I could refer to someone as "a great teacher and friend" – implying perhaps that the individual was both a great teacher and a great friend..so the positive "great" reinforces both 'teacher' and 'friend'.

AMBIGUITY: SYNTACTIC

Where the word ahead of the noun is either an adjective or verb – it works either way.

> milking cows
> drinking water

So, in the first example, does 'milking' refer to a type of cow (adjective) – or does it describe the action of milking (verb)? In the second example, does 'drinking' describe a type of water (adjective), or imply an action (verb)?

As with all ambiguity, if used deliberately it opens up thinking and greater conscious or subconscious awareness in the listener – and it can be a source of humour, and creative thinking.

I was in the bathroom this morning, thinking about buying some shaving cream – and had an image of trying to shave cream. This led me to think how delicate that operation would be, which in turn led me to think about how, as a business, in these economically challenging times, we might be able to 'cut' costs without damaging what's important....

a

ANALOGUE MARKING

One of the two types of <u>tag marking</u>. In emphasis, the delivery is fixed, delivered as a single tone shift, as opposed to sliding (see also <u>digital marking</u>).

> Sit
> > **down!**

> > > down?
> > Sit

Vocally, there is a clear and distinct change in inflection and tone in both the above cases. So the intention (command or invitation) is clearly marked, or tagged by a single change in tone and emphasis between 'sit' and 'down'.

ANCHOR

Trigger or stimulus that prompts a particular response.

A word, gesture, change of pace, sound, touch, place or setting. A tune, smell, voice or photograph. All can trigger a feeling or memory – good or bad - which then affects behaviour. The trigger may be intentional or unintentional, and the 'receiver' may be aware or unaware of its impact.

I have three pieces of music which I have deliberately chosen as mood anchors.
> *Calmness: Beethoven's Piano Concerto No 5, 2nd movement*
> *Harmony, peace: Mozart's 'E Tutti Contenti' from 'The Marriage of Figaro'*
> *Energy, motivation: 'Nessun Dorma' from Rossini's 'Turandot'*

Once they existed as recordings, on my laptop or on disc to play in the car. Now they are fully internalised, in my head, instantly available whenever I need them.

I also have <u>visual</u> anchors, pictures created from my own past experiences, which I can recall instantly whenever I wish to create a particular state. Examples include:
> *Success: myself crossing the finishing line of the London Marathon*
> *Relaxation: lying on a warm, sunny beach with the soft sand under my hands*
> *Courage: feeding sharks as a scuba diver in the Bahamas*

11

ARTFULLY VAGUE

Using words and phrases in a vague, general way that allows and encourages the other person to fill in the detail that suits them. As such, it avoids <u>contamination</u>.

> How's things?
> So.....(pause)?

This is a key concept from the <u>Milton Model</u>. In essence, and critically, the coach wants the other person to create something meaningful to themselves – something from their past or present, that is relevant to them. The more open and vague the questions, the more the other person has to create the information – the 'fill' – for themselves. So in a pure Milton-based conversation, the detail, and thus the relevance and significance, is driven by the other person, not the coach.

I have used a mind map approach, based on this concept, which has proved very successful. Knowing in advance that the other person has booked time with me to see if I can help them with an issue they are concerned about, I ask them to take a sheet of blank paper, and put their main issue in a circle in the centre. From then on I ask them to extend their issue, and their understanding of it, outwards from this centre, until they reach some possible solutions. Often, that's all it takes – and I have no idea what their issue is, or what their solutions are – the content is entirely theirs, and very free of any contamination from me.

a

ASSOCIATION

Being in the action, rather than watching yourself in the action.

> Go back to a time when you were cross with your sister;
> picture it; now....are you there with your sister, feeling
> how you feel, in the moment, in the picture....?

Usually the coach will ask the other person to "recall a time
when....", and once the other person has done that, the coach will
typically ask 'are you there, taking place in the event (associated),
or watching the event as if an observer (disassociated)?' Being
associated, rather than disassociated, can be more powerful, by
taking that person back to the actual event and placing them in the
event itself, so that they can recall the event as if re-experiencing
it. Even though they know, at a conscious level, that the event is
in the past, by re-entering it, it can create strong emotions, some
of which may have been buried or lying dormant until the event
is revisited in this way. For some, this 're-experiencing' may be
too powerful, which is why disassociation is also helpful, and
sometimes necessary.

ASSUMPTION

A view or interpretation of the world that is not evidenced by pure and unequivocal facts; a perception as much to do with the person's interpretation of the event as the facts of the event itself.

> I assume you don't like me because you haven't phoned or didn't sit next to me in the restaurant
> I assume you are clever because you went to a 'posh' school....

.t is difficult to live in the world without making assumptions – life is far too short to check out everything we <u>experience</u>: we have to make assumptions to a large extent. Some of these, based on experience, will be valid and accurate, but some will not, and are not based on experience of that individual, but on prejudice, bias and categorisations. The least we should all do is recognise that we are often making assumptions, and (worse still) that we often assume that these assumptions we are making are facts, when they are not. (see also <u>generalisations, distortions and deletions</u>).

One of <u>NLP's</u> key <u>presuppositions</u> is that 'the map is not the territory'. We all make assumptions about the world we live in, and build our own 'maps' to represent that world, and guide us through it (the map can be <u>conscious</u>, but (powerfully) is often <u>unconscious</u>).

On holiday recently, my wife and I fancied a coffee, so we went to the hotel bar. I needed to collect something from our room first, and my wife said "I'll order two coffees and a wine". I don't drink alcohol, so I knew the wine was for her. When I returned, she had ordered her wine and two filter coffees. My coffee of choice is latte, and I was SURE my wife knew this; however, she always drinks filter coffee, and she heard 'two coffees' as 'two filter coffees' – so that's what she ordered. Our maps of coffee failed to coincide....!

a

AUDITORY

One of the 5 senses in the representational system (<u>VAKOG</u>), to do with sound

> how people speak, their tone, pace and volume;
> rhythm and tempo
> music and other sound stimuli
> awareness of background 'noise'

I was working in an Art Gallery, and wanted somewhere to eat for my lunch. I couldn't see any signs for a café in the Gallery, so started to head for the exit, to go into town to eat....then I heard the clatter of cutlery, so followed the sound....to a lovely café upstairs (the sign for the café was small, and part way to the café on the stairs....)

AUDITORY CONSTRUCTED

Part of the <u>eye accessing cues</u> vocabulary; if the other person's eyes are looking to their right, neither up nor down, they are often hearing something yet to occur, in their future.

> hearing the crying of their as yet unborn baby
> hearing the wedding bells of their approaching marriage

AUDITORY REMEMBERED

Part of the <u>eye accessing cues</u> vocabulary; if the other person's eyes are looking to their left, neither up nor down, they are often hearing something from their past.

> hearing the school bell, and the dread it produced
> hearing the squeal of brakes as they recall the crash they were involved in

b

BELIEFS

**A fundamental (and often <u>subconscious</u>) value, idea, or view
of the world that typically influences or drives that person's
thoughts, emotions and behaviours.**

> belief in a God, or fate, or luck
> low or high belief in self
> belief that 'life's not fair', or 'life is what you make of it'

This is one of the most important aspects of <u>NLP</u>. An individual's
set of beliefs can dominate their lives since in effect they are
the triggers (or <u>anchors</u>) for everything that person thinks, feels
or does. This becomes even more important when the belief
or beliefs are unconsciously held – unknown – since, if they are
unknown, the individual cannot choose to have them or not, and
therefore cannot easily change: they are prisoners of their belief
systems. Of course, not all beliefs have a negative impact; but
some do, and often an individual will need firstly to challenge
and change their beliefs if they are seriously wanting to change
their approach to life, and their behaviours (see also <u>self fulfilling
prophesies</u>).

*Sometimes someone will come up to me after a course, and say
how much they wished they could do what I do – "run my own
business, do the kind of thing I want to do, love my work" (etc). I
always offer to spend time with them, to discuss how they could
go about this. In almost every case, they then say "no – I can't". I
pause for a couple of seconds, then say, "you're right!", and turn
to walk away....they always come after me, disappointed at my
apparent lack of positive support. So I then say, "how can I help*

you if you say you can't? In order to do any of this, you first have to believe you can do it. If you say you can't – then it doesn't matter if this is true or not. The fact that you believe it to be true will stop you from even starting...."

"There are those who believe they can, and there are those who believe they can't. They are both right" (Henry Ford)

b

BLOWOUT

---

see Exaggeration

Exaggerating something the individual habitually does/needs so they become averse to it.

> eating cream cakes
> avoiding making initial contact in social settings

The technique is to take the issue (eg the person wants to stop eating cream cakes) and blow it up (exaggerate it) out of all proportion, so that it becomes extreme in that person's imagination - ridiculous or distasteful, or both.

For example: "imagine you could only eat cream cakes, for the rest of your life; that you had to eat a cream cake, every hour, every five minutes, every minute - as though your life depended on it. Think of it; you haven't properly finished one, and you have to start another. You can still feel the cream in your mouth, and sticking in your throat. Your stomach is full of sloppy, messy crumbs and cream, and you are starting to feel nauseous, and to retch...but you can't stop..." (and so on).

b

BRAIN

The part of the body where mental activity takes place. The hardware that allows the mind (the software) to do its work. Can be divided into different parts, each of which controls a different aspect of individual emotion and behaviour.

what's inside the skull

The brain is where the 'neuro' part of neuro linguistic programming takes place. The brain/mind is the mothership for each individual, controlling and managing the rest of the body's internal and external reactions.

The brain is often described as consisting of several parts, each of which regulates different emotions and behaviours within the individual. These different components of the brain may be developed differently in different individuals, which makes each person more or less susceptible to particular behaviours and emotions. Despite this susceptibility, NLP suggests that we can each do a lot to take control of these susceptibilities, so that we each can do as much as we can to control our emotions and behaviours, rather than leave them to take control of us (see also mind).

Imagine you are lying in bed, asleep, alone, in the middle of the night. You are in your bedroom upstairs in a two storey house. You are woken by the sound of breaking glass, coming from downstairs in your kitchen. Someone is breaking in! You listen intently and hear the kitchen back door open and close, and then the door into the hallway open. You hear the creak of a footstep on the stair, and....then see the handle to your bedroom door slowly turn....

What <u>state</u> *are you likely to be in? Nervous, panicked, diving under the duvet?*

Now, imagine exactly the same set of circumstances happening, only this time, you had too much to drink the night before, and are actually lying deeply <u>unconscious</u> *in your bed. Your* <u>conscious</u> *self doesn't hear a thing.*

Are you likely to be in the same state?

No. And the reason is – your brain/mind has been anaesthetised and disabled. So even if your body is still able to respond, it needs the 'go' command from your brain/mind. The body will only respond to the commands given to it from the brain. And the brain will only send those commands once it has received its signals from its main processor – the mind. We need to perceive a threat before we act on it (which is why so many drunks do irresponsible things....the mind is no longer thinking clearly, and cannot co-ordinate the various bodily functions well enough....).

C

CALIBRATION

Assessing an individual's typical set of behaviours, appearance, demeanour and language, and noting any change in these which may provide insight into a particular trigger or possible internal <u>state</u> change in the individual.

> change in colour (flushing, blushing, going white)
> change in behaviour (fidgeting, looking away or down)
> change in tone and pace of language (going quiet, speeding up)

It's important to calibrate the individual's 'typical' <u>state</u> first, so that you can detect a change, and consider what might have provoked that change often by the coach explaining to the other person that they have noticed a change, and then asking them if such a change indicated anything. The coach has to be careful not to <u>mind read</u> or make an <u>assumption</u> about a motive or reason that might not be true...(see also <u>eye accessing cues</u>).

I was working with Shelley and talking about her lack of respect for managers. At one point I sat back in my chair, with my hands behind my head. Shelley visibly reacted; she tensed up, sat back in her chair, and looked annoyed. I changed my position back to how it had been before, and she immediately relaxed. I described this sequence of events to her, and she said: "That's amazing. When you sat back in your chair like that, with your hands behind your head, you reminded me of a previous manager, who was awful. And that's exactly how he sat. I hadn't realised until now how strongly he had affected me, in a negative way, and how powerfully I'd associated his negativity with his seating posture" (see also <u>anchors</u>, <u>state management</u>, and <u>rapport</u>).

CAUSAL MODELLING (LINKAGE)

Words that imply a cause-effect relationship.

> you are like this, so you can...
> you do this, and you will also do...

This may be true, factually, or it could be part of the <u>Milton Model</u>, creating an expectation in the other person's mind that it is true, or at least possible.

The main application of this idea is in transference – ie once someone can be shown they have a skill in one area, they can then see the possibility of transferring – ie of using that skill in another area.

I was working with a young student who insisted they had a poor memory and couldn't remember anything (which, in his view, was why he was struggling at school). I knew he was a keen football fan. So later, when we were chatting about other things, I asked him if he'd watched his favourite team play last weekend. "Of course", he said. "Do you know what the score was?" He looked at me as if I was mad: "yeah, he said, 2-0 to us" "who scored?" – he told me their names, instantly. "Do you know who the team was last weekend?" – he rattled off all the players names, and their positions. We carried on this conversation for a while, as he showed me more and more of his knowledge about his team. At the end, I said: "So what's all this about having a poor memory, then?"....

Of course, people tend to remember things that affect them, and/ or that they are interested in....(see also <u>reframing</u>, <u>cause-effect...</u> <u>secondary gain</u>).

24

CAUSE-EFFECT

One thing causes another thing.

> as you relax, you will discover that...
> because you have all you need, you will then work out..
> because you are studying X you will find that Y...
>
> I am not very clever because I failed all my exams
> Because my parents were not very loving towards
> me, I find it difficult to love anyone
> Because I was an only child I find it difficult to form
> relationships

The 'cause-effect' principle (sometimes known as x causes y) is a key element of the Meta Model, and distortions in particular.

Cause –effect can of course be true, and it can be implied – helpfully or unhelpfully. Much of what we call science is built upon cause-effect: water, nutrients and light cause plants to grow; gravity causes apples to fall to the ground.

In human behaviour and relations, things may not be so clear.

In the first set of three examples given above, the coach is inferring (suggesting) a relationship between one thing and another that might be helpful to the other person. The coach is suggesting that because the individual already has one component, it will lead (automatically?) to the other, desired component. So it is putting the (potential?) causal relationship into the other person's mind, perhaps making it easier for the other person to understand, accept and achieve the new and improved desired outcome.
The second set of three examples represent the unhelpful nature

of 'cause-effect'. In each example the person is making a false connection between one thing and another. This is particularly damaging and limiting, because the first thing (the cause) cannot be changed. So if the individual believes that y is dependent on x, and x cannot be changed, then it follows that y cannot be changed either – so the individual is stuck: stuck because of the false premise of x causes y.

A useful challenge to this false thinking is to ask: "can you think of any situation where x does not cause y? " For example, can you think of any only child who is able to form loving relationships? Can you think of someone you think is clever who didn't succeed at school?

CHOICE

The freedom to make a positive and empowering decision from two or more options.

> preferring to do A rather than B

The key point here is that, for choice to be valued, then at least one of the options has to be positive for the individual. It is not much help to that person if they are offered two options, neither of which is helpful or valued.

Ultimately, of course, we all have choices. And the most crucial choice we have, in my view, is the choice of our response to circumstance. We often cannot choose what happens in the world, but we can choose our response to it. And we can (if we wish, and have sufficient self-control) to choose always the most positive response. Yet many people seem to want (and wait for) the world to be different; and when it isn't to their satisfaction, choose a response that doesn't work well for them, that isn't particularly helpful....

CHUNKING

Taking the starting point, and creating new 'chunks' of information associated with that starting point, in order to create greater clarity or insight.

Chunks can be larger (chunking up – <u>Milton Model</u>, making things vaguer) or smaller (chunking down – <u>Meta Model</u>, for example challenging distortions) or <u>chunking</u> across (creating an associated analogy through <u>metaphor</u>).

After the second world war, there were lots of airfields (literally) that fell into disuse. The Ministry of Defence (MoD) asked a lawn mower company to design a new mower to keep these fields neat and tidy. Initally the lawn mower company looked at designing a new lawn mower, big and powerful enough to mow the grass in what had recently been airfields. Given the definition of the problem, this is (naturally) what a <u>lawn mower</u> company would do. However, someone then 'chunked up' – and suggested that the problem was less one of 'lawn mowing' (after all, they were talking fields, not lawns), and suggested instead a solution that would be based on 'grass cutting' (a vaguer, more generic term which would of course include lawn mowing, but also other forms of 'grass cutting'). At this stage, shears, scythes and (most creatively), sheep were discussed as possible solutions. The discussion was then 'chunked up' to the next abstract level: surely the problem wasn't one of lawn mowing, or even grass cutting, but actually 'ground maintenance'? Under this newer, more generic chunk, other solutions were suggested, including weedkiller and concrete/tarmac. In the end, the MoD decided on a joint solution of concrete/tarmac and sheep grazing – and the contract for a new lawn mower was cancelled....which is why chunking up, *which tends to lead to newer, fresher solutions, is unlikely to be suggested by those with a vested interest in the status quo – in this story, by the lawn mower company! Which in turn, is also why outsiders are sometimes brought in to companies to not only provide a fresh view and insight, but also to challenge the (restrictive) vested interests of those committed to the continuation of the status quo....*

CIRCLE OF EXCELLENCE

A technique to anchor a positive state by 'stepping into' the (imaginary) circle.

> Imagine a circle on the floor; visualise it; load it with positive energy; now, step into it and feel....

A simple and useful tool to provide you with quick empowerment and positive thoughts. And, being imaginary, you can take it with you and use it wherever and whenever you want.

COMPARATIVE DELETION

Missing standard of evaluation; a lack of comparison: a statement of scale which lacks comparison.

> my children are not very bright

Part of the <u>Meta Model</u> and a sub set of deletions. Often someone will offer a comment which they take to be true, without offering any evidence – in the example used above, the statement is without any reference point. It is taken by the speaker as a given, a truth; where on closer examination, it might not be true at all. The 'truth' depends on the reference point, and is therefore subjectively defined. For example, if the reference point is Mensa IQs of above 150 – and the two children in question have Mensa-rated IQs of 100, then that offers one 'truth'. If the comparison was against the national average of Mensa-rated IQ of 70, then this will offer a different 'truth'.

A common example of this occurs with perfectionists. Their own reference point (often unexpressed, and sometimes <u>unconscious</u>) is that of 'perfection'. Since, in almost all human activity, perfection is unattainable, perfectionists tend to beat themselves up as 'inadequate' or 'not good enough', and carry this self-image around as if it were a truth.

Chris was about to start taking his GCSE exams that week, and was very low in confidence: "I know nothing". So I asked him to open his laptop and put in all his subject headings, and then the key topics he'd studied under each heading. I then asked him to start wherever he liked, and say what he knew about any of those topics. He frowned at me, and said: "this won't take long, then". He chose a topic, and I started to type what he knew under that heading. Black text for 'sure' knowledge, and red text for 'I think so...but may need to check..' An hour and a half later, we had 26 pages of information, the vast majority of it black. "I know more than I thought", said Chris, smiling. He sailed through his exams.

COMPLEX EQUIVALENCE

One thing means the same as the other thing.

> he's an American, which means he will....
> he didn't sit with me, so he doesn't like me
> she didn't send me a text so she's forgotten about me

Sometimes referred to as x = y, another key part of the <u>Meta Model</u>, and in particular tackling <u>distortions</u>.

This should not be confused with <u>x causes y</u>. In this case, x = y, so x is the same as y – they share the same <u>meaning</u>.

So in the final example above, 'she didn't send me a text' is taken to mean 'she's forgotten about me'. The failure to send a text did not cause her to forget about me (that would be x causes y).

So x = y really is about someone choosing evidence (selectively) to create or reinforce a particular meaning.

In fact, there could be all sorts of reasons why she didn't send a text, which has nothing to do with 'forgetting'. She may have lost or mislaid her phone; she may have had no charge left in her phone; someone was on the line at the time; she may have forgotten to take her phone with her....

When John was dating Janet, they shared texts every day, and he expected Janet to text him as usual. The day passed, without a text. John became increasingly agitated. He sent Janet several texts, without getting any reply. By 6pm that evening, he was convinced his relationship was over, that Janet no longer loved him, and that she had found someone else. No texts from Janet came that evening, and John, ever more convinced, had a sleepless night, wondering where it had all gone wrong.

The next morning, at 11am, John received a text from Janet.

"John, I'm really sorry"

("Oh oh", thought John , "here comes the brush off...")

"...I had to go to hospital yesterday, because I fell over and had a nasty bang to my head. They kept me in overnight, and I'm now at home, having gone by the office to pick up my phone, which I'd left behind when the ambulance took me to hospital...hope you are all right"

CONGRUENCE

When two or more elements or features are aligned or in harmony.

> Body language matches the spoken word
> An action or behaviour is consistent with that
> person's values

Often a coach can <u>calibrate</u> the other person's behaviour and body language to check whether or not it is consistent with what they are saying.

CONJUNCTIONS

Using connecting words such as 'and', 'before', 'while', 'as'... the purpose is to state a <u>truism</u> and link it to what you want them to consider, or to the <u>state</u> you want them to create for themselves.

> we will be sitting here and having a really good time...
> while you sit here you will find out...

This is also a form of <u>mind reading</u>, where the coach is implying they know what will happen, or what the other person will think.

CONSCIOUS

Known; mentally aware, and can be recalled and identified.

> A lot of the external world, and a lot of the person's internal state and experience (but not all)

We know what we know – and we don't know what we don't know. We have two major states – the conscious state, and the unconscious (sometimes call subconscious) state. Whatever we have experienced in life, has entered our being in some form or other – through one or more of our senses (see also <u>Rep System</u>).

Some of this stays as part of our conscious self – we stay aware of it, and its effects; we can remember it, describe it, recall it, and are aware of its impact on us (makes us happy, sad, etc). But that is not the totality of our <u>experience</u>. Some experience stays in the unconscious or subconscious and though, by definition, we are not conscious of it, it still exerts a massive influence on us (see also <u>unconscious/subconscious</u>).

CONTAMINATION

Infecting someone else's view with your own.

> "don't you think that it might be due to....?"
> "you know, I think that the reason you are doing that is...."

This is something all coaches need to be aware of – the danger of putting their own views forward, which consciously or subconsciously influences the other person's thinking and reactions.

Firstly, a coach should be very self aware, and recognise both their own preferences, judgements, maps and <u>assumptions</u>. Then the coach needs high self control, to prevent these <u>consciously</u> or <u>unconsciously</u> affecting the dialogue or relationship.

One easy control against this fault is to use open questions rather than statements. A question will automatically seek the other person's view, whereas a statement usually contains your own view, as coach.

CONTEXT

The setting or environment in which the event or situation takes place.

Home, work, the past, the present....

The significance of context is that people may well behave differently in different contexts. What may be a limiting belief in one context, disappears in another context. A set of behaviours which are dominant in one context, are not used at all in another context. An expectation someone might have in one context isn't expected in another context.

As a trainer, I can spend a lot of my day talking and sharing ideas – ie engaged in dialogue. When I come home, I tend to be quiet, feeling I have talked quite enough for one day. As a result, people who know me in a domestic setting tend to see me as quiet.... which is unlikely to be a view shared by those I've just trained...!

CONVERSATIONAL COMMANDS
(CONVERSATIONAL POSTULATES)

Asking a question that is heard as a command, so gaining the response wanted without issuing a direct instruction.

> can you <u>describe your situation</u>?
> can you <u>explain how you feel</u>?

In both the above examples, the 'command' element of the question is underlined.

Asking a question is a softer approach than issuing a command.

Questions:
- offer choices to the other person
- invite (rather than insist on) a response
- sound polite, inclusive, 'other-centred'

As a consequence, the other person feels well treated, and is in a better state to respond positively to the question. As proof, imagine replying to the above two examples as questions.....then consider replying to just the underlined section (ie instructions). Do you/would you feel different?

DEEP STRUCTURE

The full linguistic representation held by the individual – ie what is restored when you get rid of deletions, distortions and generalisations.

> Everything from the individual's <u>experience</u> that is in either part of the <u>conscious</u> or <u>unconscious</u> self and, to that extent, capable of the possibility of being accessed. This includes forgotten memories and events

Firstly there is the <u>experience</u>; then the deep structure – the full impact, of everything experienced, on the 5 senses; then there is the individual's description or memory of it – the <u>meaning</u> they give to it – which is the <u>surface structure</u>, and is full of <u>deletions</u>, <u>distortions</u> and <u>generalisations</u>.

This is why two (or more) people can share the same experience (facts) and yet take different meanings from the experience. As soon as any of us experience anything, we have to give meaning to it. And the meaning we give is full of, and dependent on, deletions, distortions and generalisations. (see also <u>structure</u> and <u>surface structure</u>)

DELETION

Leaving information out (<u>consciously</u> or <u>unconsciously</u>); not taking account of the 'full' picture.

> choosing to ignore evidence that does not fit with my beliefs; being absent minded or forgetful
> being over-focused on one aspect, at the expense of others

Deletions are part of the <u>Meta Model</u>. Deletions are inevitable. Life is too short to provide a full narrative of our life, our thoughts, our feelings, our experience. When someone asks you 'how was your day?', you summarise – massively. To recall all of it (even if your memory was up to it) would take the full day (by definition), and that would just be to describe the events as they happened, You would then have to allow even more time to offer a commentary – ie to answer the question 'how' was your day.... Instead of all that, you probably say: "fine – how was yours?"

What's important in <u>NLP</u> is that people can make significant deletions – deliberately or accidentally, <u>consciously</u> or unconsciously. For example, we don't always (consciously) know why we do something, or feel something. It is only by exploring the background in more detail that we might uncover things we were unaware of, or have thought unimportant, until they are brought to light and given a full examination.

Deletions are important in another way, too. Since it is impossible to recall, let alone explain, the fullness of our experiences, we summarise, and in so doing, may leave out (accidentally or otherwise) vital information – information that provides fuller insight into the situation. As a result, we make <u>assumptions</u> based on the 'short story' which over time, becomes 'our truth'. The richness of the detail is missing, and it sometimes this detail that is significant.

My experience of watching old first world war film footage was to have seen them only in black and white. I was shocked the first time I saw events from that era in colour – it's as if I had assumed that the world then only existed in black and white!

This can not only be a problem for the story teller, as they rely more and more on the assumptions generated by the shortened story, but is also a potential problem for the coach, too. In listening to the other person's story[1] the coach is in danger of filling in the gaps from their own interpretation and experience, thus giving their meaning to someone else's story....

I was working with Sue, who was struggling with self-confidence. In particular, she felt she was 'unworthy' of the relatively senior position she held in her organisation. We talked for quite a while about possible reasons for this. We'd already had a three hour conversation in our first meeting. This was our second meeting. After an hour or so, I happened to ask her this question: "have you ever felt you have disappointed someone, or let someone down?". Sue looked taken aback, and went quiet for a while. Then she started to cry, and told me about a critical incident in her life, which had happened over 20 years ago. We discussed this in some detail, and she identified it as a significant influence – 20 years on - on how and why she felt so inadequate in her current role.

In our previous four hours' worth of discussion, this incident of 20 years ago had never been mentioned. Yet it seems to have had a significant impact on Sue's life. For whatever reason, it had been 'deleted' from her narrative.....

[1] I'm using the word 'story' throughout this book to mean 'a person's version of events'. I don't meant to imply they are 'telling tales', but rather that any (conscious) recollection of an event is, by definition, incomplete, and in that sense, only one version of events – ie 'a story'...

DIGITAL MARKING

Sliding/variable scale of marking (as opposed to fixed – see <u>analogue marking</u>).

> Eg slider switches or knobs on and audio or lighting deck.. (can turn it up or down...)

I once worked with Stefi, who was troubled by distractions and noise. She shared a house with several students, and they all shared a communal living area/kitchen. Stefi liked others' company, but found the constant chatter from other housemates very irritating as background noise when trying to read or get on with some work (but she didn't want to go back to her room, where she felt lonely and isolated). I asked Stefi what she would like to do, what she would like to see happen. She replied that she would like to turn the noise down. So she developed a mental 'slider', which had two controls: one, on her left, to turn the external noise down (or up), and the other, on her right, to turn her concentration up (or down). By playing with both sliders, either simultaneously or separately she was able to 'set' her controls to levels that suited her....

DISASSOCIATION (OR DISSOCIATION)

The person watching themselves in the action, rather than being in the action

> choose an event from your past (or future); can you see yourself in that event, as if you were watching a film of yourself, from a seat in the cinema...?

This term is usually paired with <u>association</u>. If you are associated, you are in the action, live, as it happens. If you are disassociated, you are not live in the action, but watching yourself in the action. Either term – disassociation or dissociation – can be used.

Disassociation can provide two important benefits to helping someone understand and deal with an issue. Firstly, by being disassociated, the person is safe; it is less traumatic watching a robbery than being robbed. Secondly, you might notice different things....things you weren't aware of at the time – thus providing additional insight.

As one of my fundraising activities I skydived. I also had a member of the skydiving team take a video of me as I 'fell to earth'. During the skydive I was fully associated, in the event. I could feel everything happening – how my face went like Wallace's in Nik Park's cartoon, due to air pressure, and how wonderful the coast below looked – and the shock I felt between my legs as the big parachute opened, and put a huge break on my descent (no one told me about THAT!). Later, I watched the video, and at that moment I was disassociated from the event – I knew I had experienced the dive – that it was me in the video – but I felt strangely detached, and could also see other things – about the event, and about myself, that I couldn't see from WITHIN the event, when it was happening…. For example, although I FELT the jerk as the parachute opened, when watching the video I SAW myself shoot upwards out of sight of the camera – as if I'd been shot upwards by a cannon. It's these two sensations (the associated feeling and the disassociated visual 'shooting upwards') that together give me a full memory of what it was like when the 'chute opened….

DISTORTION

Misinterpretation of information.

> putting a spin on information, either accidentally or
> intentionally; presenting a partial or biased picture

Another key term in the Meta Model.

As with deletion, it is almost impossible not to distort information.
Because we have to be selective in what and how we recall
experience, then that information gets squeezed, shaped,
transformed, to fit either the time available, or the picture/story
we want to tell.

Again, as with deletion, what's important is what gets distorted,
and why. Sometimes the person is consciously distorting,
manipulating the story or narrative; sometimes it is entirely
unconscious. And in the latter case, the unintended distortion
can create a story for that individual which is unhelpful. So by
unpicking the distortions and by taking a different view of events, a
different interpretation, meaning and perspective might emerge –
one that is equally valid, and more helpful to the individual.

*I was working with Neville, who had for years felt incredibly guilty
and had nightmares about a boating accident which put both his
children in danger. His entire story focused on 'how he nearly
drowned his children'. The story was always told from that point of
view. I then replayed the story back to him, with the same events
in the same sequence, but this time emphasising his positive
actions, which had actually saved his children from drowning.*

Neville was very quiet for some time, then said: "I've never seen it like that". I asked him to replay and repeat the event in his own words, from this 'saving' perspective, which he did, and I could <u>calibrate</u> *the changes occurring in his face and voice, as both became lighter and stronger. He emailed me two months later, to tell me that the nightmares had stopped.....*

DOUBLE BIND

Giving the individual a choice from two (or more) options, each of which will lead to the same (required/desired) end result.

> you might concentrate better by sitting or standing
> you can work on your own or in pairs
> shall we meet before or after lunch?
> do you want to tidy your room before or after tea?

Part of the <u>Milton Model</u>.

This technique seems a particular favourite of parents!

A double bind sets up a 'win-win'. The other person gets to make a choice, which gives them a sense of control; and the coach is happy with whichever choice is made, since either option delivers the desired result. Most people prefer to be given a choice, since it feels much better than being told what to do, and being given an ultimatum, which inevitably creates resistance.

When I begin my Practitioner programme, I emphasise that the learners have choices about accessing the material provided, to suit their preferences. They can either read from the recommended reading list, or read my own workbooks (including this one), or listen to my series of 40 audio files. I clearly don't mind which they do – they will all produce the desired result of 'accessing key information'

DRILLING DOWN

Probing for further details, especially when the other person is offering <u>deletions</u>, <u>distortions</u> or <u>generalisations</u>.

> always? All the time? Can you think of a time when this wasn't true?
> can you think of another reason why he might not have phoned you?

This process is particularly associated with the <u>Meta Model.</u>

Drilling down is the term used to probe for more information, for more detail, and to challenge false thinking and <u>assumptions</u>.

In conversation, people leave a lot of detail out, which might be vital to a better understanding – for themselves, as well as the coach. Often the individual makes assumptions, which can helpfully be challenged. People can get stuck in their ways of thinking – making an assumption which, though false, becomes their perceived 'truth'.

ECOLOGY

See <u>alignment</u>.

EMBEDDED COMMAND

Think of the suggestion you want to make, then wrap/package it into a sentence

> as you <u>let yourself go</u>, you..
> when you <u>relax</u> and...
> as soon as you <u>finish your dinner</u> you...
> you will <u>find the solution</u> as you...
> it seems as though <u>you can start</u> by...

In the above examples, the underlined words are the embedded commands.

Embedded commands are most often associated with the <u>Milton Model</u>, and an example of <u>indirectness.</u> If the coach simply used the command, in its naked form, it would seem abrupt, brusque, bossy. By embedding the command into a typical, ordinary sentence, the 'edge' is taken off, and it sounds less directive. The other person is less <u>conscious</u> of the command and thus less resistant to it, at a conscious level.

e

EMBEDDED QUESTION

Where the command is embedded in a question rather than a statement

> how would you <u>see a way forward</u>?
> how would you <u>put a plan together</u> for this?
> Do you feel ready to <u>make a decision</u>?
> Would you like to <u>turn the problem into a solution?</u>

In the above examples, the underlined words signify the command.

The purpose for using embedded questions is much the same as that for using <u>embedded commands</u> – they are in effect, the same device, but embedded commands tend to be statements, whereas embedded questions are, in effect, commands delivered as questions.

Embedded questions are perhaps even more powerful than embedded commands, because (generally speaking) people are less resistant to questions. At face value, a 'question' is inclusive, an invitation to respond. Yet hidden within it is an imperative. In a sense, an embedded question is a wolf in sheep's clothing....!

EXAGGERATION

See <u>blowout</u>

EXPERIENCE

Everything that impacts upon the individual – the life he or she has lived. The facts of that individual's life – everything that has happened to that individual, and which cannot be changed.

you are reading this statement. That is now part of your experience – just like it has been your experience to read many hundreds of thousands of words during your lifetime so far.
Every day of your life is your experience.
These things have happened; they are facts; they are absolute; they cannot be changed.

Experience 'just is'. It is what has happened to you, in the fullness of your life. Experience consists of objective facts, which cannot be changed. Therefore, you cannot change your experience. What is crucial, however, is the sense we make of that experience – the meaning we give to it. And that CAN be changed. Many people who struggle in life do so because they have given unhelpful meanings to their experiences. (See for example, the story provided under 'distortion'. Neville had given a meaning to that event, that was his interpretation of the facts, of what had actually happened – his experience. However, the facts – the event – the experience – were capable of being given different meanings, possibly more helpful to Neville.)

Too often, people assume experience and meaning are the same thing, as if glued together: they are not. A key to personal improvement and change is to recognise that whilst the experience is a given, the meaning is not. We cannot choose or alter the experiences we have had; we can choose and alter the meaning we give to them (see also meaning).

e

EYE ACCESSING CUES

Ways in which an individual's eye movements can reveal thinking patterns.

see the diagram at Appendix A

There are 6 'positions' that the eyes can have, and each represents a different thinking pattern, as follows (all descriptions are from the other person's point of view – ie how they are moving their eyes, from their perspective):

Up left:	visually remembered (ie past)
Up right:	visually constructed (ie future)
Level left:	auditory remembered
Level right:	auditory constructed
Down left:	internal dialogue
Down right:	kinaesthetic

Evidence for this is patchy, and may be a <u>generalisation</u> rather than a 'rule'. Also, it may differ if the person is left handed (however, I am left handed, yet still look up left to remember something – which is probably more to do with how I see time – and my <u>time lines</u>...)

Eye accessing cues are part of <u>calibration</u>. How the other person uses their eyes in dialogue may give the coach insight into how that person is accessing information.

FAST PHOBIA CURE

Way of getting someone with a phobia to re-experience a phobia-creating experience mentally, from a safe place, using a disassociation technique, leading to removal of that phobia.

> fear of a particular animal (eg spider, rat, snake)
> fear of being with others
> fear of flying

Different practitioners will use this technique in different ways, but typically the technique consists of the following steps

1. reassure the other person that the technique/process is safe
2. have the other person sitting comfortably, with feet firmly on the floor
3. ask them to close their eyes, if it helps them focus/concentrate
4. ask them to recall a time when they were faced with their phobia – ie recall an event where the phobia occurred
5. check whether they are immediately <u>associated</u> or <u>disassociated</u>
6. if associated, ask them to disassociate themselves. The usual method for this is to ask them to imagine they are in a cinema, and to come out of the film, to find a seat in the audience, ready to sit watching themselves in a film (first disassociation)
7. check they are in this first disassociated position
8. then ask them to be in the projection booth in the cinema, watching themselves sitting in the audience, ready to watch the film (second disassociation)
9. check they are able to hold the first and second disassociated positions

10. then ask them to run the film of the phobic event forward, in black and white, and when it is finished, end on a blank, white screen. They should be in the projection booth, watching themselves in the audience watching themselves on screen

11. when the film finishes (ie when the phobic event is over, has passed, and they have 'survived'), check they are OK

12. then ask them to switch from black and white to colour, and to run the film <u>backwards</u>....and as they do so, recall all the events, but in reverse order

13. get them to do this process several times, and each time, ahead of the backwards run, make them make the event more extreme – eg by making it faster and faster, using <u>sub-modalities</u>, and by <u>exaggerating</u> sound effects/music, visuals (eg costumes), voices and dialogue (usually humorous). The overall and cumulative effect should be of a technicolour 'keystone cops' or cartoon movie, which makes the person with the phobia smile

14. once the coach has <u>calibrated</u> a change in <u>state</u> in the individual, from anxious to smiling, from tense to relaxed, end the process

This technique needs skilful handling, and will not work for everyone. When it does work, however, it has a powerful and lasting effect. The technique works through the following <u>NLP</u> principles and applications:
Disassociation: the individual is twice removed from the event, which is recalled from the past (via the 'film' <u>metaphor</u>); so the position is safe for the individual – it isn't happening now, live –

and of course, the individual has 'survived' – another safety net.
Positive <u>contamination</u> through <u>sub modalities</u>: the rerunning of
the video backwards and forwards adds new and dramatic sensory
information, which dislocates the individual, breaking up their
'assumed' and fixed view of the phobic event
<u>Anchors</u>: the new sensory information provides new anchors –
ideally positive and humorous (ie non threatening and nothing to
be feared – in fact, more likely to make the person laugh or smile),
so that when a new event or situation occurs in the future, which
could potentially be phobic, the individual will have a different
'past experience' to remember, which may change their state from
'fearful' to 'relaxed and happy'

As a result of the above, the individual has a different, more
positive map of their phobic territory...

FILTERS

The various 'frames' we use, subconsciously, to see the world.

> The Representational System (Rep System) (VAKOG)
> RAS
> Memory
> Metaprograms
> Meaning

No two people will interpret the same experience in the same way. Two people reading this glossary will take different things from it. This is because we all 'see' or interpret things differently (not better or worse, right or wrong – just different).

> "The map is not the territory"

So we filter any experience through a range of devices – our previous experiences, and what they have meant to us; our general awareness and sensitivity levels; our interest (what we choose to focus on/be interested in); our balance and mix of senses (eg whether we are more visual or auditory); our biases and prejudices, and our memory, which can be fallible (we forget things, and we mis-remember things....). Given all of this, it is a wonder that any of us share the same or similar views of anything...!!

Being aware of these filters, how they exist within us, and the impact they can have on our interpretation and understanding of ourselves and our world, is one of the main contributions of NLP.

FRACTIONATION

Starting one story, then breaking off into another story, and perhaps another, before eventually completing them all.

> I want to tell you about A......
> But before I do, here's something about B....
> Which reminds me about C....
> Anyway, as I was saying about A....

Billy Connolly and Ronny Corbett are experts at this...starting a story, wandering off into something else, then coming back..

In NLP terms, the purpose is twofold. Firstly, it encourages the listener to think, and to keep an open mind, and concentrate. So it has a similar purpose to puns (see ambiguity) in that the brain has to keep several 'channels' open, and hang on to more than one idea. Secondly, it is a form of indirectness, in that, by leaving a story 'hanging', the coach is encouraging the listener to complete the storyline themselves - ie fill in the gap..... (see also nested loop).

FRAGMENTATION

As coach, sounding hesitant and failing to complete a sentence, as if struggling to recall information....and so encouraging the listener to complete the sentence/find the information themselves.

> so, the point I'm making is...that....er....
> so that's called...oh, what's the word....

The aim of the coach, in using this technique, is to encourage the listener to concentrate and fill in the missing elements themselves. So it is a form of <u>indirectness</u>, encouraging the listener to work hard and fill in the gaps....

FUTURE PACING

Asking the other person to check whether an idea or solution will work in the future, by checking it against their <u>Rep System</u>, before they do it for real.

> look ahead and see yourself..imagine yourself having...
> how does that look? How does that sound? How does that feel?

By asking the other person to check ahead, into the future, the coach is essentially asking the individual to confirm the idea or solution's <u>ecology</u> – ie that it will work for them in all aspects, and not have any unwanted side effects. It also makes the solution or idea seem more real, through checking it in this way. Asking them to systematically check their <u>Rep System – their VAKOG</u> – ensures thoroughness, and avoids the coach and the other person making an <u>assumption</u> that an idea that seems good in the present will inevitably work in the future. The process also allows the coach to observe the other person doing this, and thus <u>calibrate</u> if there are any noticeable changes. Finally, going through this process is part of ensuring the idea or solution is a <u>well formed outcome</u>....

g

GENERALISATION

Coming to conclusions about other situations from a single situation.

> everybody....
> you always....

Another key part of the Meta Model.

As with distortions and deletions, generalisations are very common. We cannot, in reality, know of every circumstance, so we generalise. We have a single piece of information, or evidence, and unless we are very careful, we assume that what happens for one person in that category, happens for everyone in that category. Or what that person does once, they will always do. Or, in terms of the individual's own behaviour, they assume that because they were once like that, or behaved in that way, then they are forever going to behave in that way, or 'be like that'.

> "That's just the way I am"
> "I can't help it"

"It's in my genes – I was born like this"
"A leopard cannot change its spots"

Generalisations create rigidity, inflexibility – and thus stop the individual from exploring and being open to new options and ideas. Generalisations are part of an individual's <u>self-limiting beliefs</u>.

Generalisations are relatively easy to challenge, by the coach asking the other person to find an exception to the rule:

When I was taking my own Master Practitioner course, my coach asked me to identify an issue I wanted to improve, to discuss with her. So I chose the issue of clumsiness. I often used to describe myself as clumsy – ie bumping into things, knocking things over... My coach recognised the generalisation I was making, and sought for exceptions to invalidate it: always clumsy? all the time? She asked if I played any sport, which I did (squash, badminton, rugby), and asked if I regarded myself as 'clumsy' in these sports. This, for me, was a real lightbulb moment. I said, "no, of course not" (The idea of being clumsy in these sports was preposterous to me – how could I play any of these sports and be clumsy??) The coach just sat back, and allowed me to invalidate my own generalisation about clumsiness for myself. Since I was therefore only 'clumsy' in some <u>contexts</u> but not others, then clearly clumsiness was a behaviour option or <u>choice</u>, and not a genetic defect.... This therefore allowed me to work on improving my clumsiness (choice, behaviour) rather than see it as a self-defining fixture (<u>self limiting belief</u>) (See also <u>secondary gain</u>)

g

GODIVA CHOCOLATE PATTERN

A technique to encourage the other person to associate with a positive experience from their present/past, and thus be more open or receptive to a new idea or solution.

> where is your favourite place? So, imagine you are there...
> what do you most enjoy doing to relax? OK, so imagine
> you are doing this...right now....

The technique gets its name from the fact that (apparently) Godiva Chocolates were regarded as 'the best available', and thus would always be associated with excellence.

The name of the technique doesn't matter – what's important is the use of the tool to create a positive <u>state</u> in the mind of the other person. Of course, it is important to let the other person choose their form of 'Godiva Chocolate' – it could be a place or activity (as in the two examples above) or it could be any <u>VAKOG</u> – sound, feeling, smell, taste....

g

GUSTATORY

Referring to physical taste in the mouth.

> sweet, sour, acidic, citrus, sickly...

Gustatory – a taste – is one of the five senses of the Rep System (VAKOG).

Many people have a strong physical sense of taste, and the (positive or negative) recall and association with such tastes can create powerful anchors for their behaviour.

Sometimes, when training, I will ask if anyone can recall the taste of medicine. Most of the group will react with quite dramatic body language by screwing up their face or moving their head back, as if in recoil at the memory. The same can happen if you mention school dinners....

HOMOMORPHIC METAPHOR

See 'metaphor: homomorphic'.

h

HYPNOSIS

An altered <u>state</u>, a form of <u>trance</u>, which can either be self induced or induced by the coach, and can be accidental or deliberate, and in which the person becomes less and less aware of their <u>conscious</u> state and surroundings.

> daydreaming
> fantasising
> 'drifting off'
> watching a movie
> listening to a story

An hypnotic state can range from the everyday <u>experience</u> of 'daydreaming' to being induced by a coach into a deeply hypnotic state.

The word 'hypnosis' can be a threatening <u>anchor</u> to some, so it might be best to refer to the hypnotic state as a form of trance, which most people can relate to.

In any trance, at any level, the individual loses contact with 'consciousness' to some degree. In <u>timeline</u> terms, they move from the present, to either the past, or to the future. So one purpose of hypnosis, or trance, is to help the individual access their past, or project their future, by removing them from (an awareness of) the present.

A range of relaxation techniques, classically including meditation, help create trance states.

Regular and rhythmic patterns of any type can induce a trance – hence the unfortunate impact of strobe lights on some (the same effect can be had if driving along a road which has evenly placed trees alongside – the light through the trees can produce a similar effect, resulting in trance-induced, hypnotic accidents...). Trancing can also commonly occur through vocal patterns...intended or otherwise:

When I was a lecturer, a student of mine had a very young baby, and normally arranged child care for when she had to attend class. However one week she asked me if she could bring her baby in to class, as she had been unable to arrange child care for that day. I said "yes, of course". She promised that if her child was disruptive in any way, by crying, for example, she would of course leave. She attended the class with her child, and there was no disruption – the baby didn't make a sound. At the end of the session, the student came up to me, with the baby in her arms, and said "That was fantastic: as soon as she heard your voice, she went straight off to sleep..."

INDIRECTNESS

Leaving things vague, unspecified, so that the other person fills in the detail for themselves.

> Telling a story or offering a quotation that the listener makes relevant for themselves

Indirectness is very much part of the <u>Milton Model</u>. By being indirect, or vague, the coach reduces the <u>assumptions</u> built into his or her own comments

I've recently been working with a national museum, that (informally) uses a lot of NLP principles and practice in making its displays and interpretation helpful to its audiences. One way it does this is through its use of posters and quotations. Part of the gallery walls will contain a poster or quotation – with no 'added' explanation or interpretation: it is for the visitor to make up their own mind as to its relevance and <u>meaning</u>....

INDUCTION

Methods for creating a <u>trance</u> or <u>hypnotic state</u>.

>Gazing into a flame
>Watching a film
>Reading a book

I find it easy to create self-induced trance: by gazing into the fire, or flames, or watching a candle flicker and burn; or by gazing at the clouds in the sky. By removing my 'self' from an awareness of the external world, I find it easier to go 'in' to my internal world, and begin to access thoughts, feelings and ideas that I would otherwise not access in a more <u>conscious</u> state...

INOCULATION

Creating a <u>context</u> and <u>state</u> for the other person (or group) so they are less likely to have unhelpful expectations and feelings

> some might have an idea that...but most people find
> that...
> before we begin...

To take each of the above examples in turn:

"Some might have an idea": sometimes an individual or audience may have a sceptical mindset to begin with – for a number of reasons (eg reputation, previous poor <u>experience</u>, general anxiety about the unknown). This technique recognises and acknowledges concerns that others have felt (thus reassuring the listener that 'they are not alone'), and then <u>reframing</u> the expectation into further reassurance that there is nothing to fear. This technique is helped if the phrase moves from some (= a few) to most (= the majority) – as in "Some may have thought that the language of NLP is too difficult, but in fact most have found it eventually easy to understand and helpful to use".

"Before we begin...": as a course tutor, I often use this phrase as a form of inoculation. "Before I begin" sends the (<u>unconscious</u>) message for the listener that "I (the listener) can stay relaxed, because the serious stuff hasn't started yet". So the more obvious barriers of anxiety can be lowered....making the listener more relaxed and open to the learning. (In fact, I never say "OK, we are beginning now..." – why would I!)

When I started as a trainer, I was often faced with a group of participants looking quite stern and unenthusiastic. For some time I wondered what I had done wrong, or why they had taken an instant dislike to me. I soon realised from experience that the reason for their unwelcoming state was their anxiety. Not just a general apprehension about the unknown, but specifically, more often than not, a fear of being picked on, of having to speak in front of the group, of being made a fool of – all of which often came down to two words: role play! To test my theory, when I next encountered a group displaying this state, I said: "before we begin, just one announcement. There is no role playing, and no-one will be asked to do anything they don't want to do" The effect was immediate – like they'd all been wearing tight corsets or belts and had just had them loosened....(An easy <u>*calibration*</u>*)*

INTERNAL DIALOGUE

A conversation the individual has with themselves, mentally.

> "I'm not going to do that – it won't work, and I'll look a fool..."

The term 'internal dialogue' is actually a bit of a misnomer; a more accurate phrase would be 'internal monologue'. This is because, in most cases, there isn't a balanced dialogue going on in the person's head – it's all one sided. Most frequently the internal conversation is a negative, unhelpful one, emphasising what could go wrong or why any solution or idea wouldn't work.

The real trick is to be aware of this internal conversation, and its limitations, and make it more of a balanced conversation. The way to do this is to put a positive option/alternative against each of the negatives that come first.

INTERNAL REPRESENTATION

See 'Representational Systems'

IN TIME

Where time is seen as a line which passes through the individual, from entering the back of the individual and exiting from their chest

> future ahead, past behind, living in the here and now

This is one of the two classic <u>timelines</u> (see also <u>through time</u>).

Using in time, the individual is <u>associated</u>. The individual has a sense of being 'present' in and on their own time history. For some, the in time timeline also gives a clearer sense of separation: what is ahead (the future) is not only more clearly separated from their past (which is behind them); it also has a powerful <u>metaphorical</u> impact – ie 'the past is behind you; look ahead to your future; concentrate on that'

ISOMORPHIC METAPHOR

See 'metaphor: isomorphic'

KINAESTHETIC

Referring to the physical sense of feeling/touching.

> holding, grabbing, stroking

One of the five senses of the <u>Rep System (VAKOG)</u>.

Some individuals are very tactile, and this can be <u>calibrated</u> through their use of gestures/body language, and the words they use. Others may be <u>kinaesthetic</u> in their need to be active, to be doing things. They value movement, and may be good with their hands (or other parts of their body – as are actors and dancers).

1

LACK OF REFERENTIAL INDEX

Unidentified pronoun, so the 'owner' is unknown (ie not referred to)

> it can't be helped
> we're all the same
> they're out to get me

This is part of the <u>Meta Model</u> in general, and <u>deletion</u> in particular.

In each of the above examples, the question is who or what, exactly, are we talking about? What is the 'it'? Who is meant by 'we'? Who precisely are 'they'?

Probing questioning can reveal more detailed information, and help the other person clarify what or who they mean. (Also, by being more specific, the individual reduces the <u>generalisation</u> they are in danger of making...)

Avoiding responsibility and ownership by leaving out the doer or person responsible. This is classically the territory of the blamer – someone who avoids personal responsibility for either their situation, and/or doing anything about it.

I was working as coach with Sophie, who had a low self-image. She felt uncomfortable, as in too heavy, and said "my weight has gone up; my clothes are too tight". By using this language Sophie had no sense of personal responsibility for the weight or tightness issue. The way she used this language, it sounded as though the weight and the clothes are responsible for the problem.... Consider the difference if instead Sophie had said: "I have put on weight, and I am now too large for my clothes". In both cases, the 'I' makes it clear who is responsible for the situation, and who needs to take action. Of course, such a statement feels more uncomfortable for the user – exactly because the ownership is now clear...! (See also <u>linguistics</u>*).*

There can be a particular common problem with 'it'.

> it's unfair
> it's difficult
> it's not easy

When someone refers to 'it', they can often mean 'I'. The impersonal style of 'it' removes personal ownership, and places the problem 'out there', owned by the world, rather than 'in here', owned by the individual.

I ran a training course once on 'Time Management'. One of the participants – a senior manager - had three key issues he wanted me to address: an untidy desk, which cost him time to sort out each day; too many interruptions, and too many competing priorities. I offered a number of solutions, which he was very pleased with. A month later I visited his company again, to run a different course, and went for my lunch in the company restaurant. The senior manager was at a table with colleagues, and as soon as he saw me, he called me over and asked me to join him. He introduced me to his colleagues as "the trainer who ran a marvellous course on time management". I was of course, delighted. He then spoiled it rather by saying: "unfortunately, it didn't work." I asked him why that was, and he said that despite attending, he still had the same three difficulties. What I wanted to say, of course (but didn't) was that rather than "it didn't work", perhaps the problem was that "he didn't work at it". The 'it' was hiding the 'I'. (He then went on to say, "so when are you running it again, so I can attend again..." Hmmm – I don't think 'attending' is the problem...)

l

LINGUISTIC

Language and non-verbal communication systems through which neural [representations (VAKOG)](#) are coded, ordered and given [meaning](#).

> what we say (and don't say), and how we say it: words, tone and body language

This is the 'L' of [NLP.](#) As such, it is a central component and underpins much of NLP's principles and practices.

Whole books can and have been written on this topic, and it is not the function of this glossary to go into the many ways NLP uses language and language patterns to create positive [states](#) in others, be more persuasive and help others gain greater understanding and control of how they relate to others and themselves.

However, I think two elements of linguistics are crucial, and worth mentioning here: the what and how of communication.

'What' refers to the content – the facts, the information, the knowledge that someone wants to provide.

'How' refers to the way in which that information is provided – the skills, processes and patterns used; the words and tone chosen (deliberately or accidentally).

Often individuals spend time on the what, rather than on the how. Both are equally important – in fact, some would argue the how is more important, since the 'how' is often accessed ahead of the 'what'. Put another way, the 'what' is always packaged in some form of 'how', and as with any product, the packaging both influences the user or purchaser's first impression, and also makes it easier or more difficult to access the information or product it contains. So when communicating, think packaging as well as product.

Judith, a participant on a recent Practitioner programme, had given a presentation to a group of midwives. The presentation fell flat, and none of the audience accepted the key points being made. Judith reflected on why the presentation had been received so badly, and concluded there was nothing wrong with the message (content) but how it had been presented. She felt that the way she presented the material used her language preferences, and a style that suited her – rather than the audience. Judith had another presentation to make, putting the same messages across, to another midwives group. She kept the messages the same, but changed her style and language of delivery. The presentation was a success, and this group of midwives fully accepted and enthusiastically endorsed Judith's key recommendations...

l

LINKAGE (CAUSAL MODELLING)

See 'causal modelling: linkage'

1

LOGICAL LEVELS

Different categories of information, arranged in a hierarchy or concentric circles, and intended to help the individual identify the level (or levels) that have most significance for them.

The logical levels are:

> Spirituality/world view (eg religion, mission in life)
> Identity (eg sense of self)
> Beliefs and values (eg sense of right or wrong; moral code)
> Capability (eg skills, abilities)
> Behaviour (eg key actions and habits)
> Environment (eg conditions, surroundings, setting, context)

These logical levels can be used, analytically, to help the individual identify where current blockages or barriers exist. Using the levels as a checklist, the individual can be encouraged to examine whether there is anything about their environment, behaviour, skills, beliefs, sense of self and spirituality that needs to be challenged, investigated further and/or improved.

Issues do not always fall neatly into any one of the levels, but instead may cross several of them. For example, I was working with someone who was struggling with a particular relationship. During our discussion, it was clear that this difficulty could be usefully examined in terms of the impact of the setting where the difficulties occurred, key behaviours that affected the relationship, lack of key skills from both parties, assumptions and beliefs each had about the other, and a sense of low self esteem resulting from the relationship....

1

LOST PERFORMATIVE

A statement of fact or value judgement which excludes or omits the source of the assertion.

> girls develop faster, intellectually, than boys
> schoolchildren today just cannot concentrate

This is another example of the <u>Meta Model</u>, and <u>distortion</u> in particular (though it is also an example of <u>deletion</u> and <u>generalisation</u>, too).

In both the above examples, the key question is: "says who?" There is no authority or source quoted, and so an opinion is stated, as if it were a fact. As a result, such statements become generalised assertions. Even if it were true, there would be exceptions –so a more accurate statement might be 'most girls....' or (more likely) 'some girls...'.

A useful question from the coach would be: "can you think of any examples where this would not be true – for example, can you think of a pupil you know whose concentration is good?" Using language in this way can create categories, labels and stereotypes, all of which can be unhelpful.

In terms of self-image, lost performatives can be damaging. Individuals can tell themselves 'I am no good at....' without any evidence to back this up – or worse, ignoring evidence to the contrary...

I was working with a talented woman – Elise – who, despite a lot of evidence to the contrary, was very self-deprecating in her use of language, and always emphasised what she could not do, rather *than what she could do. She rarely, if ever, had any evidence for what she couldn't do, and continued to ignore the evidence of what she could do superbly well. It took a lot of time and energy on my part to help her – not only recognise her strengths, but also to realise how her self-deprecating, lost performative language reinforced her low self-image – and might impact unhelpfully on others. I explained that for some people – including perhaps Elise – such negative self talk can have a <u>subconscious secondary gain</u> – ie positive reinforcement and external validation. People like Elise might (subconsciously) use self-deprecating language to trigger a positive reassuring response from other people – "oh no, you're really good" – "that's not true; look how often you..."....etc). When I mentioned this possibility to Elise, she didn't like the implication (for her) of 'seeking approval', felt it would be judged as manipulative. She immediately changed her style of language, being far less self critical, and much more balanced in her self evaluation (and hence self-image)....(see also <u>linguistics</u> and <u>lack of referential index</u>)*

MATCHING

Creating and sustaining <u>rapport</u> through being more 'in line/in sync' with the other person.

Body posture, tone and pace of voice

When two people are 'getting on' and empathetic towards each other, they will often 'harmonise' through their body language and vocal patterns. Walk into a pub, and look around: you will often be able to see who really gets on with whom, and who is isolated in any group – by observing body language and listening to conversations (do this discretely!). Often two people who are attracted to each other will mirror each other's body language.

We do all this unconsciously, because we have learned, as humans, that we 'like people who are like us'. So when we match someone else, or they match us, there is an implied affinity, a 'coming together'. So we have learned to 'read' matched behaviour as an indication of compatibility, of being liked, of being comfortable in that person's company.

All of the above is <u>unconscious</u> behaviour. A coach can take <u>conscious</u> advantage of this aspect, however, by deliberately matching the other person's body language and tone, in order to create (implied) affinity and compatibility, to put the other person at ease, and create a more relaxed and trusting environment. And if in any conversation, the other person matches your behaviour and vocal patterns, it probably means they are comfortable with you....something useful to <u>calibrate</u>....

Whenever I visit any part of the UK that has a strong regional accent, I find myself unconsciously adopting that accent. I suspect this is part of wanting to fit in, to match the local population – to be in sync, to be in rapport....

MEANING

The interpretation given to any event or <u>experience</u>

> The dog barking is being aggressive
> The dog barking is being friendly

In the above example, 'the dog barking' is the event or experience; 'is being aggressive' and 'is being friendly' are different interpretations of the same event or experience – different meanings given to the same experience.

"Man is a meaning making machine" (Richard Bandler)

Whatever we experience, we have to make sense of it – we have to give it meaning. But the meaning we give to it is ours, personal to ourselves. Two people will not necessarily give the same meaning to the same, shared event – because we are all unique, and uniquely different – we have each travelled a unique and personal journey through life. So although an experience can be shared, the meaning derived from that experience is likely to be different for each person sharing that experience. So though territory may be the same for each of us, each of us will create a different map....and then run our lives according to the map, rather than the territory. So we will run our lives according to the meaning we have given to our experience, rather than the experience itself.

There is also one other difference between 'experience' and meaning': the experience cannot be changed – but the meaning given to the experience can be. The experience is objective, fact: the meaning is subjective, opinion. Too often an individual will assume the experience + the meaning given to it are both 'objective, fact', and therefore that neither can be changed. Whereas the important reality is that the experience cannot be changed, but the interpretation of it can be (see the example of Neville quoted under '<u>distortion</u>'...)

I work with Geraldine, who will often ask me for my opinion on something, then, whatever I suggest, she will challenge and criticise it. Initially, I was deflated and frustrated by this, and could not understand why Geraldine was bothering to ask my opinion, since she clearly didn't value what I had to say. One day I challenged Geraldine on this, and asked her why she bothered asking. "Oh," she said "I really DO value your ideas and opinions. My challenges to your ideas are my way of thinking your idea through...". I realised I had given a different meaning to the experience. Now I understood the purpose behind Geraldine's challenges. I could and did alter the meaning I gave to them, and was much more comfortable with them from then on...

METAMIRROR

see <u>perceptual positions</u>

Taking each of 4 positions (perspectives) in order to see things differently

> self
> other person
> observer
> both of us

So in any two-way conversation, there are four positions/ perspectives that can be taken. The first position is that of yourself – how you see what's happening. The second position is that taken by the other person – so consider how things seem from that person's perspective – how do they see what's happening? The third position is that that would be taken if there was an observer in the room, watching yourself and the other person (the typical 'fly on the wall' position) – so how would what's going on look to a neutral, third party perspective? And the fourth position is that of a possible 'shared' perspective, coming from both yourself and the other person. What would it look like if both parties shared a view?

Using the metamirror approach encourages us to look at a situation from different vantage points, each of which is likely to provide a fresh perspective, and possibly better understanding.

I used to do quite a bit of acting in my younger days. I was once playing 'Fagin' (in the musical 'Oliver!') in a live performance, when something really strange happened. I became aware of what I can only describe as an 'out of body experience'. I was clearly 'Fagin' the character, consciously fully immersed in the role; and yet – at the same time – I was aware of me, as myself, watching me perform. I was about two feet away from my 'Fagin' self, to Fagin's left. I was simultaneously able to look at the stage, the other actors, and the audience, through Fagin's eyes, and also, as me, floating in space, look at Fagin's performance, and the impact it was having on the audience. I was both spooked and excited by this newly discovered ability, and as a coach, have been able to use this skill to apply the metamirror technique. So whilst staying as myself-as-coach (first position) – I have been able to detach myself to look at the event through the other three positions....

META MODEL

The process of probing the other person's statements, to drill down for more detail. Often associated with tackling and challenging <u>deletions</u>, <u>distortions</u> and <u>generalisations</u>.

> who says?
> how do you know?
> always, never, every?
> what do you mean by that?
> compared to what, who?
> who, what, where, when, how?
> specifically?
> what stops you?
> what would happen if you could...?
> how do you know when you do that?
> can you explain...?

The Meta Model is essentially used to search for greater detail and clarification. So the main contribution by the coach is to ask questions, and to do so in a non-threatening, non-aggressive and non-interrogatory way. So the tone of the coach's voice will be important, and it may also be helpful to preface the question with softening phrases such as:

> I'm curious to know.....
> That's interesting, so I wonder....

Given that we all delete, distort and generalise (both <u>consciously</u> and <u>unconsciously</u>), it is important for the coach to recognise when any of these three features are present, and then look to find greater evidence and detail, to provide both the coach and the other person with greater understanding and insight. The coach also should recognise the need to probe for clarity and understanding, rather than make their own <u>assumptions,</u> and fill in the gaps from their own perspective (see also <u>meaning</u> and <u>mind reading</u>)

METAPHOR

Stories or incidents that convey the message you want to give, without it directly applying to the other person – so they make the connection for themselves.

> Fairy tales
> Aesop's fables
> 'Who Moved My Cheese?'

The use of metaphor is a powerful tool in <u>NLP</u>, and is most often associated with the <u>Milton Model</u> and <u>indirectness</u>.

Story telling is an ancient art, and is a very powerful way of grabbing attention. People like stories. Since however it is a story and therefore about someone or something else, the listener/ audience can relax – because it is not about them. So they have no defensive barriers, and are open to what is being said – and often/ usually enjoying the experience....at the <u>conscious</u> level.

However, at the unconscious level (and sometimes at the conscious level) the story begins to resonate for the listener, who translates the story into their own experience: it connects.

So the use of metaphor can be a very effective way of getting a message across and through to another person. The story gets their attention: the punch line (the moral of the story) gets them connected.

One of my team, Diane, and I have written a book called 'Are You Sitting Comfortably?'. It contains 52 stories, each acting as a metaphor for personal learning and development. They work at one level as simple stories, but they are also metaphors, in that they implicitly are meant to extend the readers self-awareness and insight into their own attitude and behaviour...

Many of the examples (in italics) in this book are metaphors....

METAPHOR: HOMOMORPHIC

Generalised application.

a story about feeling happy or positive...

A homomorphic metaphor is one that is intended to address a general condition or emotion, applicable to most people. For example, stories about happiness, determination, courage, making decisions, etc that would be relevant for most people.

m

METAPHOR: ISOMORPHIC

Specific to an individual listener.

> a story about someone having an aversion to frogs...

An isomorphic metaphor addresses a specific condition or issue, which is relevant to fewer people – and so is more likely to resonate to that individual, but also likely to be seen more consciously by the individual as a story directed at them.

METAPROGRAM

A 'big picture' framework or model of the world (map) which shapes how we think'.

> towards/away from
> proactive/reactive
> big picture/detail

As in the above examples, metaprograms are often presented as contrasting pairs, mainly to show quickly and easily how each pair provides a contrasting view and interpretation of the world. For example, someone who has a 'big picture' preference would most likely want an overview first, before the detail; someone who has a 'detail' preference would want the detail first....

So a metaprogram is in effect a <u>filter</u>, through which someone views the world. Someone's metaprogram (or metaprograms – they can have more than one) represents their preferred way of accessing or presenting information.

Each person's unique <u>Rep System</u> (their combination of <u>VAKOG</u> preferences) is part of their metaprogram: some people, for example, will have a strong <u>visual</u> filter or preference; others might have a stronger <u>auditory</u> filter.

In <u>NLP</u> terms this is important in how it contributes to creating <u>rapport</u> and being persuasive. If I want to persuade a client to accept a solution, it's really helpful to know if they have any metaprogram preferences, so I can match them. Using the above example, if my client is a big picture person, then it will help if I begin by painting an overview of the situation, and possible solution – then move to the detail later. If, on the other hand, I started with the detail, they are more likely to disengage and get frustrated: I'm not working with their preferred metaprogram.

Charles was, to put it bluntly, quite an arrogant man. He was English, and had a view that the British currency was well respected – and accepted – throughout the world. Charles decided to take a holiday in Greece, but refused to take any Euros (the host country's currency), taking instead his spending money in pounds sterling. When he returned, I asked him how he had got on. "It was a nightmare", he said. "You would not believe the trouble I had getting shops and bars to accept my money. They often refused, and got quite cross. They seemed not to understand that my money was every bit as good as theirs. In the end, in desperation, I changed the money I had left into Euros – and things became much, much easier after that...."

In effect, a metaprogram is like a currency (the word we prefer to use when we are training or coaching). If you want to create rapport and be positively influential and persuasive, it is important to work in the other person's currency, rather than your own....to match their metaprograms, rather than your own.....

MILTON MODEL

A set of processes and tools associated with Milton Erikson, to create conditions and statements which are <u>artfully vague</u>, imprecise and <u>indirect</u>, so that the other person has to fill in the detail themselves, and thus make the detail (and <u>experience</u>) relevant to their own world. The following are all regarded as components of the Milton Model:

> <u>truisms</u>
> <u>quotations</u>
> <u>vagueness</u>
> <u>metaphors</u>
> <u>trance</u>
> <u>fragmentation</u>
> <u>fractionation</u>

Just as the <u>Meta Model</u> is used to drill down, looking for detail, the Milton Model works in the other direction, opening up the other person to a range of interpretations and possibilities by deliberately creating and using vagueness. So the coach, using the Milton Model, will be as vague as possible, thus encouraging the other person to fill in the detail from their own experience. So one of the great benefits of using the Milton Model is that it reduces the coach's likelihood of <u>contamination</u>.

The examples given above are all techniques compatible with the Milton Model, in that they create indirect, vague or in complete information, encouraging the other person to fill in the details themselves.

As a coach, working with someone who has booked a session, but not told me what it is about, I will often begin with one of the following:

so...what would you like to talk about?
so...what's on your mind?

Both statements <u>presuppose</u> the condition mentioned – ie that they want to talk, and there is something on their mind. That is reasonable, given they have booked to see me...about something. But keeping it as vague as I can ensures that the topic or issue for discussion is theirs, led by them, described by them, and relevant to them.

I was asked by a colleague, Katie, if I would have a 1-1 coaching session with her sister, Sandra. Before I could intervene, Katie told me what she (and Sandra) thought Sandra's 'issue' was: Sandra was an actress, and had real difficulty in controlling nerves. I agreed to meet with Sandra. Katie was at the time on my Practitioner programme, and asked if she could sit in on my 1-1 with Sandra, to observe coaching in practice. With Sandra's permission, I agreed.

I met Sandra, with Katie observing, and started by asking Sandra what she would like to talk about. She glanced at her sister, and said, "I don't really know....Katie thought it would be a good idea if I talked to someone about nerves..." I asked her if that's what she wanted to talk about, and she said, quite hesitantly, "yes....it... is". I asked if there was anything else she would like to talk about, and she immediately became more confident, and more strident, and started to tell me about how she felt the acting profession discriminated against women, and Northern women in particular.

We spent quite some time on this issue, and only in the final half hour (of a 2 hour session) did we return to the topic of 'managing nerves'.

After the session Katie came up to me, open mouthed. "I cannot believe that I've known my sister all my life, and yet not known she had this view about the prejudice shown to her, and women, by her profession....I'm shocked at how little I know of her. I've always thought nerves was the problem...."

MIND

The 'software' to the brain's 'hardware' – the 'system' that processes and controls the way we think, feel, and react; interprets <u>experience;</u> and gives it meaning (<u>consciously</u> and <u>unconsciously</u>). Our mental <u>state</u>.

> all mental activity
> all thinking and thought
> all interpretations
> all perceptions
> the way our <u>VAKOG</u> is processed

Our minds are in effect our control centre, our 'mothership'. Almost all of what we do – certainly consciously – comes from the way our mind works. And the way our mind works has largely been influenced by our personal experiences, and our reaction to them. We need our brain as the hardware, to allow the software of our mental processing (awareness, thinking, interpreting) to take place. Each person's brain has the same components, but they are not developed in exactly the same way in each person. Some of this is due to accident – our hardware may have different configurations – but the way we each use our brain to process our experiences is a mental activity, that we can intervene in – we can challenge and change the way we think, interpret and react....which is of course why, though we all have a brain, we use it in different ways...

MIND READING

Making <u>assumptions</u> about the other person as if they were true – as if you (or the other person) were able to read someone's mind

> you are probably thinking about...
> I expect you are now curious
> you might be feeling curious and slightly unsettled, and that is ....

Mind reading works in two ways, each way associated with different parts of <u>NLP</u>.

In terms of the <u>Milton Model</u>, the coach will sometimes behave as if they can read the mind of the other person, perhaps to help <u>inoculate</u> against anxiety and help put the other person at ease. For example:

> "I know you have all you need to work this out"
> "As you work on this you will find it easier...."

So this is a form of reassurance, intended to be helpful.

Within the <u>Meta Model</u>, however, the coach's role is to probe and challenge any unhelpful mind reading exhibited by the other person. So if the other person makes an assumption about what someone else thinks, or their motive for an action, then that is mind reading:

> "I know she doesn't like me...."
> "I know what he'll say...."

I was working with Cathy, a senior marketing manager. She was working full time, but with a young family wanted to work part time. However she was convinced that 'they' wouldn't agree to this. I suggested she ask them, and find out. She said there was no point. This continued for about a month. In the meantime, even though she loved her current job and employer, she started looking for another job which would be part time, simply because she believed the answer to her preference would be no. Unable to find a job she liked, she decided she may as well ask – and their answer was an unqualified 'yes'. She phoned me that same night, to say: "why didn't I ask a month ago, and save myself all that unnecessary effort and stress....?"

MIRRORING

See '<u>matching</u>'

MODALITIES

The 5 basic senses: visual, auditory, kinaesthetic, olefactory, gustatory (<u>VAKOG</u>). Our '<u>Rep System</u>'

What we see, hear, touch, smell, taste...

In essence, each of these five senses is a mode through which we <u>experience</u> the world. (see also <u>sub-modalities</u>)

MODAL OPERATORS

Words that imply a particular way of doing things. So how someone uses/chooses key words, will, through those words, create an expectation of a particular approach, strategy or behaviour

> I have to tidy the house before my mum arrives
> I might like to go to India one day

There are two classic types of modal operators: <u>Modal Operators of Necessity (MON)</u>, and <u>Modal Operators of Possibility (MOP)</u>. (See immediately below for a discussion of each). The key point to make here is that the use of MON or MOP is a <u>choice,</u> though often it is not a <u>conscious</u> choice. But it is a powerful example of how the language we use creates expectations, which are often accidental, unintended and (sometimes) unhelpful.

MODAL OPERATOR OF NECESSITY

Words that imply an inherent necessity to do something – thus removing choice. The language is restrictive

> should, must, need, ought

People who have a MON pattern of speaking put pressure on themselves – perhaps unintentionally, by restricting choice and ownership. And of course, any failure to deliver can lead to the individual 'beating themselves up'...ie being self critical:

> I must get this done
> I have to do this before I go out
> I should be a better daughter
> I need to be better at this
> I ought to keep a tidier house

In all the above, there seems to be no freedom to choose. Clearly in most cases, the person could in fact choose other options – but the way they use language to describe the situation and themselves makes it seem like there is no choice. So they have <u>distorted</u> their reality by using MON language, and placed themselves in a straitjacket.

MODAL OPERATOR OF POSSIBILITY

**Words that imply an inherent openness about possible actions
– thus endorsing and emphasising <u>choice</u>.**

> might, like, could, maybe, perhaps, possibly

People who have a MOP pattern of speaking emphasise choice
and ownership. As a result, they are putting less pressure on
themselves, creating less of a straightjacket within which to
behave.

> I might get this done
> I'd like to do this before I go out
> There are things I could do to improve the way I relate to
> my mum
> I'd find it helpful to be better at this

By using MOP language, the individual 'opens out' the possibilities,
by giving themselves more options. And since there is no
'necessity' to do it, there is less built-in chance of failure....after all,
it was only an option, a possibility...

*I was working with Brian, who had a phobia about being in the
company of others. He had had several coaches and counsellors,
and had also received medical treatment. The phobia was deep
and engrained, and since nothing that Brian had tried so far had
helped, he was both sceptical and gloomy about the prospects for
any improvement.*

Having listened to Brian describe his situation, I asked my first question: "Do you believe you can change?" He thought about his answer for a long time, then said: "I honestly don't know...." I then said: "Do you believe in the possibility that you could change?" He instantly and immediately said: "Yes".....

MODELLING

Finding someone who's excellent, and observing closely what they do and how they do it.

> watching how Billy Connolly does what he does so well, to identify and observe skills such as <u>fragmentation</u> and <u>fractionation</u>

<u>NLP</u> has its beginnings in modelling. It's two co-founders, Richard Bandler and John Grinder, spent a lot of time observing hypnotherapists such as Milton Erickson to discover how they did what they did so successfully. So one of the key principles of <u>NLP</u> is that it is possible to observe excellence in others, distill it, copy it, and achieve similar results.

n

NEGATIVE COMMANDS

Giving a command in a negative context, so that the listener cannot think of a negative without first thinking of the positive ("don't imagine a blue elephant").

> don't *think deeply about what you are learning..*
> you don't have to *accept everything I am saying...*
> it isn't necessary to *work everything out...*
> you don't have to *be clear..*
> *it isn't necessary to start feeling relaxed, open and confident*

As with many NLP techniques, this can be used helpfully or unhelpfully.

In a positive sense, a negative command can encourage someone to think first of the positive – as in the examples above. So the positive instruction is hidden within, and by, the negative.

In a less helpful way, but following the same logic, we can ask someone not to do something, which immediately places the 'something' in that person's mind; making them more likely to do what isn't wanted. Parents will probably recognise this:

> Don't run
> Don't knock that over
> Don't spill your drink
> Don't forget to phone your nan

To avoid this, avoid negative commands. Rephrase the negative into a positive – eg:

> walk
> be careful
> take care with your drink
> phone your nan

As I've mentioned elsewhere, I have had a tendency to be clumsy. This is something I want to work on, to improve. I started, of course, by giving myself a negative command: "don't be clumsy" – all this did was put 'clumsiness' in my mind...and so I continued to be clumsy. A better command for me is 'watch where you are going'....

NESTED LOOPS

**A more sophisticated form of <u>fractionation</u>, in which the
speaker starts a series of stories, say in sequence A, B, C, D,
and completes them in reverse order – D, C, B, A – so that each
story is 'nested' or embedded within the other ones.**

A diagram can help here

Billy Connolly and Ronnie Corbett (in his story telling chair) are past
masters at this.

Nested loops are associated with <u>hypnosis</u> and <u>trance</u>, and can be
a powerful tool to help the speaker plant an idea or command into
the listener's <u>unconscious</u>. Here's how it works:

- the listener hears, and pays conscious attention to story A
- the speaker, before finishing story A, moves on to begin story
  B (and so on)
- the listener's conscious self will pick up on the new story, and
  start to listen to that; the listener's unconscious self will try to
  work out the unfinished story
- the more stories that are started, the more the listener's mind
  becomes overloaded, trying to complete stories
- then – and this is the decisive moment, the story that contains
  the main (hypnotic) message that you want to give to the
  listener, is given in the final story – the one that is started
  and completed all in one go (D in the above diagram). The

unconscious mind, wanting the previous stories to complete (A, B & C), is now very grateful for at least one of them to be completed (D), and so is very receptive to the message of story D. At this moment, the listener is most aware of D....

- The speaker then closes the other stories, which reduces the listener's conscious awareness of D, as they become more focused on C, B and A.
- So the real message, attached to story D, is now nested, or embedded, within the other three – so the listener may have little conscious recall of that story, but by being the only story that was complete at the time, is likely to be remembered best by the listener

NEURO

Nervous system in the brain through which <u>experience</u> is received and processed through the individual's unique combination of the 5 senses (<u>Rep System/VAKOG</u>).

> how we access, interpret, process, store and
> retrieve information

Crucial to anyone's attitude, emotions, <u>behaviour</u> and self image is the way in which that individual relates to the world, and gives meaning to that world. All of that is controlled by the <u>mind/brain</u> combination: the way each individual 'relates' to the stimuli they receive from the world and their experiences within it. Some of this neurology is fixed, and people are 'wired' differently. However, a lot of how each of us receives and interprets our experience of the world is down to ourselves – we can change our outlook, our perspective – we can choose what to look at, how to look at it, and what particular 'sense' to make of it. All of this happens in the mind, and this then affects the rest of our 'being' – how we think, feel and behave....

NLP

Neuro Linguistic Programming: the relationship between how we interpret the world, how we communicate about and within the world, and how we develop predictable habits that shape how we function in the world

> the way we access and process information
> the thoughts we have, and the way we think (neuro)
> the language and words and tone we use (linguistic)
> the habits we have (programming)

Everything else in this book connects to these three elements – the way we process information, the way we think, the way we communicate, and the way we behave.

n

NLP PRESUPPOSITIONS

A set of <u>assumptions</u> about the world and how we are within it, that underpin a lot of the ideas within <u>NLP</u> – ie 'where NLP is coming from'.

> eg the map is not the territory
> the meaning of the communication is the response
> you get

Here are 10 key assumptions (or principles) that NLP makes about the way people are or can behave in the world. Different authors have different lists - this is mine:

1. The map is not the territory
2. People respond according to their map of the world
3. Changing the way we see things may be more important than changing reality
4. You cannot not communicate
5. The meaning of the communication is the response you get
6. There is no failure, only feedback
7. Every behaviour has a positive intent
8. Individual worth is separate from worthwhile behaviour
9. You have all you need
10. All distinctions we are able to make can be represented through our five senses

You may or may not accept or believe any or all of the above. The key point is that the body of knowledge known as NLP is making clear some of the working principles and assumptions that underpin the subject.

n

NOMINALISATION

Turning a verb into a noun, making the description more impersonal, and open to interpretation.

there is a lack of communication

In the above example, the verb originally was 'to communicate', but has now been replaced by a noun 'communication'. So we don't know precisely what the problem is: 'lack of communication' could mean a host of things.

A coach should listen out for nominalisations, and (as part of the Meta Model), probe for further detail and clarification:

What do you mean by 'communication'?
Who isn't communicating?
What isn't being communicated?
How is the communication lacking?
Where and when?

O

OLFACTORY

The sense of smell.

> scents, perfume, fresh grass

Some people have a strong sense of smell, which can be a strong <u>anchor</u>, creating negative or positive associations.

I was once working with Anna who had a real fear of going to, or being at, the dentist. It was mainly associated with (anchored to) the smell of the waiting room.... Anna had another powerful (smell) anchor: her mother's perfume. So to overcome the negative olfactory anchor of the dentist's waiting room, Anna doused a handkerchief with her mother's perfume, and took it with her to the dentist. It worked: the more powerful positive anchor replaced the negative one....(see also <u>swish technique</u>) Of course, this approach could have backfired, in that the dentist's room might have been a strong enough anchor to overpower the perfume, with the danger that, from then on, whenever Anna smelled the perfume it would remind her of the dentist...!

PACING

Moving into synch, in step, in tune, with the other person.

> matching someone's speed of verbal delivery
> walking pace
> breathing

Being 'in synch' with the other person can help put them at ease – so a coach will often adjust their own language, style, verbal and body language to be 'in step' with the other person. Of course this can happen <u>unconsciously</u> as well as <u>consciously</u>.

Pacing and <u>matching</u> are often seen as the same; the main difference is that pacing is done as a first step to leading the other person to a different <u>state</u> – eg the coach may match or mirror the other person's quick pace before (as coach) moving to a slower pace themselves (called <u>leading</u>), hoping the other person will respond.

As a trainer, I will often use pacing and leading. For example, I may want to follow a high energy activity with some group or personal reflection. At the end of the activity the group is often 'buzzing' and excited, with a lot of noise and energy, but I would like them to be quieter, and eventually silent. I will start to pace, by talking about what's coming next at the same energy and volume level, then, as I continue to talk, will slow down, reduce the volume and energy, and by the time I hand over to the reflection activity, they will be in a different state.

PATTERN INTERRUPT

A technique used to break the other person's habit, programme or state, before helping them replace it with another more helpful habit, programme or state.

> sudden noise
> interruption with a metaphor or story
> taking a break
> asking an unrelated question

(May also be known as 'breaking state'.)

Before an individual can switch strategies, from A to B, they need to let go of the first (A), in order to be more receptive to the second (B). It may therefore help to build in a way of stopping the individual from thinking and feeling A, completely, so that there is more of a 'blank canvas' for B.

A favourite programme interrupt of mine to help people move from anxiety to problem solving, using programme interrupt, as one of three key stages: identify the current state; interrupt or break that state; change the original state into something more productive.

Firstly I ask them to identify how they know or can tell they are anxious or worried – how does this state manifest itself to them, through their Rep System. They usually tell me a physiological cue – sweat, tension in the neck or jaw, knot in the stomach, and so on. For me, it is a knot in my stomach, or stomach churn.

I then ask them to create a very strong signal, using their preferred Rep System. One I use personally is a strong flashing red neon sign, spelling the word 'STOP!' (highly visual). This is the 'breaking state' or 'programme interrupt' mechanism. I ask them to then anchor this signal to their physiological identifier for anxiety – so that every time they 'feel' anxious, they instantly recall their programme interrupt device. In my case, as soon as I feel my stomach churn, I can visualise the 'STOP!' sign.

I then create the third step, a strategy installation of a 5-step problem solving model: what's the problem; why is it a problem; what are my options; which of those do I prefer/works best; do it! I then ask the individual to anchor this strategy to their programme interrupt. So the three step process happens like this, very quickly:

Physiological cue >>>>>programme interrupt>>>new strategy

In my case:

Stomach knotting>>>>>>STOP sign >>>>>>> 5 step strategy

So I (and others who use it) are taken quickly from focusing on anxiety to focusing on problem solving. This is also a distraction technique: the brain cannot process different information consciously with the same intensity or concentration. The more you focus on B, the less you can focus on A.

When my father had his first heart attack, I was a lecturer, and needed to rearrange my teaching for the coming week. During that time, people asked me if I was worried, but I wasn't – because at that time I was preoccupied with the mechanics of sorting out my timetable. But as soon as I jumped into my car for a lone drive from Manchester to Newcastle, I was alone with my thoughts, and nothing else to think about – so I began to worry...

PERCEPTION

The way each person sees and filters 'their world'.

What do the following mean?
> fire
> flush
> mobile

Each word above has several <u>meaning</u>s:

> Fire (something burning; shoot; sack)
> Flush (a toilet; looking red in the face; a hand at poker; abutting)
> Mobile (above the cot; hand held phone; able to get about)

As soon as we sense something through our <u>Rep System</u>, we have to interpret it, give it meaning. So when you read the initial list above, you are likely to have given each word one meaning, based on your <u>experience</u> of that word, and the <u>context</u> in which it has most frequently been used. This is usually <u>unconscious</u> – we aren't aware of other alternatives, until we are faced with them.

Some of our perception is based on <u>distortion</u>; we 'take a point of view' perhaps as a <u>choice</u>, because it confirms our prejudices. Again, this can be <u>conscious</u> or <u>unconscious</u>.

Once we have perceived something in a way that gives it a meaning (deliberate or otherwise), then that becomes our 'reality', and we tend then to seek and select evidence which confirms or reinforces that 'reality', leading to further distortion.

As a lecturer, I often had to mark exam scripts. Usually this was a two person task, to help avoid bias. At this time, the name of the student was on the front cover of the answer book (this wouldn't happen today). I was marking Andy's script. He had been a student who I felt was bright, but lazy; he'd tended to do the minimum to 'get by'. One of his answers, however, was particularly impressive. I knew that my co-marker, Eric, had a downer on Andy – felt he was wasting his time and abilities. So I set up a little experiment. I handed the script to Eric and said, as neutrally as I could: "what do you think of this?". Eric, before looking at the essay, turned to the front cover of the book, saw Andy's name there, and sighed: he read only one paragraph, and said: "well, what do you expect – it's rubbish...." And they say, 'don't judge a book by its cover...'

PERCEPTUAL POSITIONS

See 'metamirror'

PHONOLOGICAL AMBIGUITY

See 'ambiguity: phonological'

POSITIONS (ALSO KNOWN AS PERCEPTUAL POSITIONS)

Different positions you can take to look at the same situation

> first – self
> second – theirs
> third – independent onlooker
> fourth - shared

'Putting yourself in someone else's shoes'. This is about looking at the same situation from different perspectives. We all typically take the first position as standard – how things look or seem to us. But it can be very useful to take the other positions – how does the same situation look to the other person – what if I were them, in their shoes, having had their <u>experience</u>(s)? Sometimes it's helpful to take the other positions too, to get a more 'rounded' perspective (see also <u>metamirror</u> and fast <u>phobia</u> cure)

POST-HYPNOTIC SUGGESTIONS

Suggestions made by the coach to the other person when the latter is in a <u>hypnotic state</u>.

> as you sit there, relaxed, you will begin to see...

Having created a hypnotic state, or <u>trance</u>, the coach offers ideas to the other person who is more receptive to these suggestions in this state.

PREDICATES

Process words like verbs, adverbs and adjectives which give a sense of that person's preferred <u>representational system</u>.

> sounds, looks, noisily, colourfully

So the language people use can be a clue to their preferred rep system, the way they use <u>VAKOG</u>. In conversation however, it is useful for the coach to ignore their own preferences, and work to <u>match</u> those of the other person (if known).

I'm a strongly <u>visual</u> person, so I often use visual language. For example:

> *Can you see what I'm getting at?*
> *How does this look to you?*
> *The picture I'm getting is....*

However, if I continue to talk in this way with someone who is not particularly visual, this is unlikely to be helpful...

PRESUPPOSITION

<u>Assumptions</u> about the other person or the world that the speaker takes to be true.

> what commitment will you make to...
> how will you create an action plan...
> how will you be more successful...
> I know some of you will be...
> once you are able to...
> what it will then mean is...

In each of the above examples, the speaker is presupposing certain things to be true ie:

> that the person is already committed, or will be
> that they will create an action plan
> that they are already successful
> that some of them will be
> that 'being able to' will happen
> that there is a meaning that will be clear

The thinking behind this, for a coach, is to place the idea into the other person's head as a reality – so the other person feels more confident, more certain...about themselves, and their future. By making a presupposition, the coach bypasses the issue of whether it is true or not, which could take time and waste time. Imagine for example that instead of presupposing things to be true and in place, the coach converted each to a question or a less certain statement:

are you, or are you likely to be, committed....?
are you going to put an action plan together...?
how successful do you think you are?
it's possible that some of you will be....
you might be able to....

These versions may create unhelpful uncertainty and doubt. Equally, it may be important for the coach to challenge presuppositions (often <u>unconscious</u>) that the other person has. Probing these presuppositions through questioning can be helpful.

The following sections all refer to particular types of presuppositions.

PRESUPPOSITION: ADJECTIVES/ADVERBS

Designed to suggest a helpful and positive process or state.

how easily, how quickly...

PRESUPPOSITION: AWARENESS

Designed to raise consciousness – often an <u>embedded command</u>.

realise, become aware, notice, learn, discover, know

PRESUPPOSITION: CHANGE OF TIME

Designed to place the thought (or embedded command) in a time frame.

> begin, end, stop, start, continue

PRESUPPOSITION: COMMENTARY

Designed to create, emphasise or reinforce positives.

fortunately, happily, luckily, obviously

PRESUPPOSITION: OR

Designed to emphasise <u>choice</u> (implying that there is one).

will you x or y?

PRESUPPOSITION: ORDINAL NUMBERS

Designed to create a suggestion of sequence.

first, second, last

So by implying 'first', it sets up the listener to be ready for a 'second, third', etc

PRESUPPOSITION: SUBORDINATE CLAUSES OF TIME

Designed to create anticipation, and sometimes to <u>alter state</u>.

before, during, after, while

(See also <u>inoculation</u>)

A good NLP trainer friend of mine, Julie, will often start her training session with the phrase: "before we begin.....". The message this sends to the group is that they can be or stay relaxed, because "we haven't started yet..." So all <u>conscious</u> (and <u>subconscious</u>) defences are down – and in fact, the learner is as a result, more open to the learning....

PRESUPPOSITIONS OF NLP

See 'NLP Presuppositions'

PROCESS

The method or approach someone uses to do something; the how, rather than the what.

how you learn, rather what you learn

Very often how we do something is more important that what we do. Two people can do the same task (what) using different methods or approaches. <u>NLP</u> usually refers to the 'how' as <u>strategy</u>.

I was working with a young boy – Kieran who was trying to learn his multiplication tables. He just wasn't making progress, and was clearly getting fed up – and started to refer to himself as 'useless' and 'stupid'. I knew Kieran well, and in observing him, I noticed how he loved his music, and in particular, rap music. I often heard him singing current rap hits to himself – word and rhythm perfect. So....I made him a 'rap tape' – rap music with the multiplication tables dubbed on top – with spaces for him to join in. Sounds cheesy? Maybe – but he had the whole set nailed within the week....The what he had to do hadn't changed – but changing the how – the process – made all the difference.

PROGRAMMING

Behaving in predictable, <u>subconscious</u> ways; habit

> folding arms
> sitting in the same place every time
> reacting in the same way to the same triggers or stimuli

This is the third component of <u>NLP</u>.

Everyone has habits – routines we follow every day of our lives. Think of your typical day – getting up, getting washed, cleaning your teeth, getting dressed, having a meal, going to work.....all of these are probably predictable patterns of behaviour, repeated in the same way, unthinkingly, day after day....

Most of these habits are <u>unconscious</u> – we aren't aware of them as habits; some of course are <u>conscious</u> – we have consciously learned them, then embedded them as habits through practice (eg driving).

These habits, or programs, to use the NLP term, can be helpful or unhelpful. One of the benefits of NLP is to make individuals aware of their unconscious, unhelpful habits, and help the individual replace them with more conscious, positive ones. A key point is that, for a habit change to be effective, the old program has to be replaced with a new one. It's very difficult for the individual to just stop. Something better needs to replace it. There is a well known four step model which incorporates the idea of programming:

Unconscious incompetence (I don't know I do it, or that I do it badly)
Conscious incompetence (I suddenly know I do it, or that I do it badly)
Conscious competence (I do it better, by making a conscious effort)
Unconscious competence (I do it well automatically, without thinking)

For many of us, driving is the best example of the above....

Steven had unconsciously learned the habit of clicking his pen top. He was unaware of this program, and also unaware of the negative impact it was having on others, who saw this gesture as a sign of Steven's irritation of disinterest (neither of which Steven intended). When Steven was made aware of this habit, or program, he immediately wanted to end it. We discussed what his motive might be for pen clicking, and he couldn't identify one, other than wanting to do something with his hands (not everything has, or needs, a motive). So instead he identified what I call a 'pattern interrupt': as soon as Steven became temped to click his pen, he interrupted the program, by creating an anchor, and consciously chose to do something else instead. In Steven's case, the anchor was a vision of the other person exploding in frustration; and his substitute program was to make sure he put his pen down, and put his hands together. (He could of course have chosen to use a non-click pen – though he then might have used it as a 'stabber'.) His 'reprogram' worked, and over time, became an embedded new habit.

PUNCTUATION AMBIGUITY

See 'ambiguity: punctuation'

q

QUOTATION

Putting ideas into the other person's <u>mind</u> by using someone else's words.

> Milton once said *"you are all you need"*
> my son once said: *"you've got to practice to get anywhere"*
> Gary Palmer said: *"the harder you practice the luckier you get"*
> Richard Bandler said: *"man is a meaning making machine"*

This is part of the <u>Milton Model</u>, and an example of <u>indirectness</u>.

The other person hears the quote, and since the quote is about someone else, they do not feel threatened by it, or a need to accept it – at the <u>conscious</u> level. Indirectly however, at the <u>unconscious</u> level, the quote is often processed for its relevance for that individual – and if it is seen to have relevance, it sticks.....and may well be quoted back at some time.

The <u>NLP presuppositions</u> are mainly in the form of quotations ie:

> *The map is not the territory*
> *There is no failure, only feedback*
> *Every behaviour has a positive intent*

Quotations also have four other benefits: firstly, they often represent or reveal someone's <u>belief</u> system – people use quotes that are particularly significant for them. Secondly, quotations are often short, and are therefore useful summaries. Thirdly, quotes can confer authority on the statement, giving it more power and legitimacy – especially if from a source respected by the other person. Finally, because of the previous points, quotes are often memorable.

RAPPORT

Creating and sustaining empathy with another person

congruent use of spoken and body language

People are more likely to be positively influenced by someone who is in rapport with them. So having the ability to spot the other person's preferences then use them, can be a help (see also programming, matching, pacing and calibration)

Sue Knight tells a great story in her book, 'NLP At Work'

In medieval times, a village was living in fear of a dragon, living in nearby fields. A knight came by, and offered to slay the dragon. He went into the field, only to discover that what the villagers had taken to be a dragon was actually a bunch of melons. Laughing, he came back to the village and reported his findings. The villagers killed him. A second knight came by, and the process was repeated, and this knight was also killed. A third knight arrived, was told about the dragon, and, like the knights before him, discovered only a melon crop. This time, however, the knight destroyed the melons, and returned to the village to announce he had slain the dragon. The village cheered, and welcomed the knight as a returning hero.....

RAS (RETICULAR ACTIVATING SYSTEM)

The brain's filtration system that selects crucial messages from all the information that's available.

3 key selection criteria are survival, novelty and emotional content

Parts of the brain are wired for survival, newness and emotional resonance, so the brain searches all data and experience for these three factors, and tends to respond to them. So anything threatening, anything new, and anything that creates emotional resonance are quickly picked up and processed – which is why we all respond quickly, reflexively, without thinking, to these three 'prompts'

REALITY VIOLATION

**Giving a concept life, or giving a person an inanimate quality –
creating something that cannot be 'real' (sometimes referred
to as 'selectional restriction violations').**

> This chair is sad
> Your confidence will carry you through...
> Your happiness will be your friend, and create
> new possibilities....

This is part of the <u>Milton Model</u>, and associated with <u>indirectness</u>.

The purpose of this approach is to make the other person 'make
sense' of the reality violation. In what way can a chair be sad? In
answering that question, the other person will have to consider
'what it is about the chair – the chair's attributes – that represent
sadness'; and also what is meant by 'sad'. These are thoughts that
are not likely to occur under normal conditions, so it is a way of
getting the other person to think in new and perhaps more open
ways. In some circumstances, it can induce <u>trance</u>, by taking that
individual's thinking into new areas, creating fresh and deeper
reflection.

REFRAMING

Representing one view – usually negative – in a more positive way.

> glass half empty, or glass half full
> problem focused, or solution focused
> "It didn't work" or "I didn't work at it"

Reframing is a very powerful tool within the NLP toolbox. The main idea is to switch viewpoints – mentally to see or experience the situation through a different frame, to allow a more positive perspective. There's an old adage: "seek and you will find", so we tend to focus on information or perspectives that we are looking for, or have been encouraged to look for. Consider the space you are in now, as you read this. Look around, and find three things that are negative about the space. Now change frames, and look for three things that are positive about the space. You can do the same for your job, family members, key relationships....anything.

Often the most effective reframes are conscious choices – where the individual deliberately chooses to look at the <u>experience</u> through a different frame, or perspective.

Donna had two young children – aged 3 and 7. They'd all been staying with friends for the weekend, and had a 50 mile drive home. The weather was forecast for snow, so they set off early. Normally it was a 90 minute trip: this one turned into a journey of ten and a half hours! This was mainly due to the car breaking down three times, and the failure of the 'emergency services' to provide helpful solutions. Difficulties experienced included: breaking down three times; being stuck on the motorway, unable to get onto the hard shoulder; a later refusal of the breakdown service to prioritise the breakdown (even though it was a car containing 3 women) – because they were in a service station, even thought it was closed;....being scared, a dying phone battery, and the tiredness of the children.

Normally Donna would have been anxious and angry, and transmitted this to the children. As an NLP student, however, Donna decided, quite consciously to reframe the journey from its negatives to its positives. So she used positive language, such as 'adventure', and 'exciting'; she kept calm and positive with all those 'trying' to help her; and played games with the children, including Donna doing press ups at 1am at the service station, as a forfeit for losing a game. As a result, there was little or no stress for the whole 10 hours, and the children – two years on – still recount the experience with real enthusiasm...

> "we had chips..... twice"
> "we played games"
> "we sat in a fire engine" (actually a rescue truck – another reframe!)

Donna says: "Change the frame, and you change the perspective. Change the perspective, and you change the mood and behaviour; change the behaviour and you change the experience. What could have been an absolute disaster, and created a negative view of travel and their mum, is fondly remembered as a key adventure, a positive experience of travel and their mum..."

Occasionally, however, a reframe occurs accidentally, and very powerfully.

I was visiting a friend, who keeps tropical fish. I asked him "Is it difficult to look after the fish?". He replied: "No – it's more difficult to look after the water". I had never considered this perspective before, and it not only told me something about keeping tropical fish, but (as a <u>metaphor</u>) encouraged me to think of the importance of environment on our individual and group performance and welfare....

REPRESENTATIONAL SYSTEM (SEE ALSO VAKOG)

The five senses through which we experience the world.

> Visual
> Auditory
> Kinaesthetic
> Olefactory
> Gustatory

(Sometimes also referred to as Internal Representations). The key point here is that each individual has their own unique blend of the above. Typically we all have all 5 senses operating, but some will be stronger than others.

This is significant in two ways. Firstly, as individuals, if we know which of our 5 senses is strongest, we can make use of this in the way we access, and particularly store, information. I have a strong visual sense, and so if I want to remember, or (literally) 'make sense' of something, I will picture it, or create a diagram of it......

Secondly, if you want to build rapport with someone, or influence them positively, it is useful to use their preferred Rep System.

I was running a training course requiring a team to solve a particular problem. The team split into sub-groups to work on their own ideas, then present them to the larger team. One sub-team of two presented their ideas verbally. Earlier in the day, another member of the team, Rachel, had expressed her preference for visuals, so I looked at her as she listened to the verbal presentation. She was clearly confused. She then stopped the speakers, and said: "I'm not getting this, sorry". So the two presenters looked at each other, then went back over what they had already said – LOUDER..!! Eventually Rachel stopped them again and said: "Sorry guys, it must just be me....I'm just not very bright...".

So I walked over to the flip chart and, looking at the two presenters, said: "Can I just check if I understand what you're saying?", and drew a diagram that I thought represented what they'd said so far. When I'd finished, Rachel said: "Is that it?". I looked across at the two presenters: they nodded. "Well", said Rachel, "NOW I understand!" In the event, the two guys' idea was the one adopted by the team.....and Rachel presented it to the panel – using diagrams, of course....

RESOURCES

Set of nine personal assets we all have, or can develop, to help us in our life.

> Open, aware, curious, responsible, flexible, creative, fun/humour, perseverance, pragmatic

These are the 9 resources that have been identified within NLP as being particularly helpful.

To help me understand and embed these resources, I created this poem:

> *I am open to being aware*
> *And curious to know what's out there;*
> *I can flex and create*
> *And responsibly state*
> *I have plenty of humour to spare.*
> *That leaves perseverance*
> *And pragmatic adherence*
> *To a toolbox that we can all share.*

RULES

A set of <u>metaprogrammes</u>, they are the expectations and boundaries individuals set that regulate that individual's judgement and responses.

> things are either right or wrong, black or white;
> live and let live;
> take every opportunity and risk

They often exist as <u>assumptions</u>, <u>beliefs</u>, <u>generalisations</u>, principles and <u>presuppositions</u>. They are, in a sense, an individual's personal 'governance' or regulatory code. Some of these may be <u>conscious</u>, and consciously chosen, some not.

One interesting consequence of rules is the issue of flexibility. Flexibility is one of the 9 key <u>NLP resources</u>, yet an individual's flexibility is often constrained (or enabled) by the rules which govern their thinking and decision making.

I was working with an NLP Practitioner group, and one of its members – Val – had a very strong rule of 'right and wrong'. Much of her language, and her opinions, were driven by this 'rule'. She would often say:

> *"that's not right..."*
> *" that's just wrong..."*
> *" the right thing to do would be...."*

As a consequence, Val often sounded very judgemental, and quite inflexible; and as a consequence of that, the group consulted her less, and were less influenced by her contributions....

S

SCOPE AMBIGUITY

See 'ambiguity: scope'

SECONDARY GAIN

The benefit gained by the individual having the problem.

> clumsiness producing quick reflexes
> being a victim producing a rescuer and avoidance
> of responsibility

One of the <u>NLP presuppositions</u> is that every behaviour has a positive intent. In other words, there is a positive outcome somewhere along the line. Very often, this intent/outcome is not known at the conscious level – but it exists, and is all the more powerful for being unconscious and therefore 'unknown'. Of course, it helps answer the question: 'why do some people persist in doing something that doesn't seem to help them?' At the surface level, that may clearly be true; but probe deeper – is there something that the individual gets as a result of the apparently negative behaviour and choice? If someone is getting a benefit, it will make it harder to change their strategy, if the new strategy does not deliver the gain or benefit. So any new strategy will also have to deliver the existing secondary gain, in order for it to work.

Under the 'generalisation' heading, I've recounted my story about clumsiness. This is a good example of secondary gain. Since my clumsiness sharpened my reflexes, which were useful for all the sports I played – I had no incentive for being less clumsy. And, if I wanted to address my clumsiness, it would have to not be at the expense of my secondary gain of sharpening reflexes....

SELECTIONAL RESTRICTION VIOLATION

See reality violation

SELF FULFILLING PROPHESY

see also <u>self limiting beliefs</u>

Associated with <u>beliefs</u>, in that having a belief makes the belief more likely to happen.

> believing you have no confidence makes it more likely you will behave with no/low confidence

Beliefs can be helpful or unhelpful, enabling or disabling. If the individual believes something isn't possible, then they are unlikely to try to make it happen. Because it doesn't happen, then this confirms the belief. But it isn't the belief that prevents it happening – its the lack of action based on that belief.

> So:
> - It's the belief that 'I can't do it' that stops the individual from taking the action that would make it happen
> - It's the belief that 'I can do it' that encourages the individual to take the action that would make it happen

Hence two people (A and B) can ideally want the same thing. A believes they can do it, B doesn't. So A takes the necessary action, and B doesn't. So A gets what s/he wants, and B doesn't. Beliefs drive actions which determine outcomes.

If someone wants a different outcome, they need to adopt different actions, which may mean challenging existing beliefs.

"Whatever we believe, we give ourselves permission to achieve"

SELF LIMITING BELIEFS

See also <u>self fulfilling prophesy</u>

What the individual unhelpfully believes about themselves and the world often restricts or limits their actions and outcomes.

> I depend on others for my happiness
> I can't remember names

This relates to, and is another form of, a <u>self-fulfilling prophesy</u>. The individual may put a limit, or brake, on their actions (and therefore their preferences) because, quite simply:

> I don't believe it can happen (the world)
> I don't believe I can do it (me)

Again, some of these self-limiting beliefs can be conscious, and some may be unconscious.

For years, athletes had tried to break the 4-minute mile barrier. In the 1940s the record was pushed to 4.01, where it stood for 9 years. Lots of athletes had come close, but none had broken the barrier – until, on May 6 1954 Roger Bannister ran 3.59.4. His record lasted......46 days.

By contrast:
> *Frederick Forsyth's 'The Day of the Jackal', which often appears on 'great reads' lists was rejected by four publishers before it was accepted*
> *Abraham Lincoln failed to be elected to the state legislature, Congress (twice), the Senate (twice), and Vice President before succeeding in each, and eventually becoming US*

President
Colonel Sanders approached 1,009 restaurants before getting a contract to sell his grandmother's recipe of 'Kentucky Fried Chicken'

None of the above suffered from self-limiting beliefs!

SIMPLE DELETION

Statement with missing or deficient information.

>Abraham Lincoln died at a theatre
>Mohammed Ali was a conscientious objector

Part of the <u>Meta Model</u>, and the most simple form of <u>deletions</u>.

Clearly, it is impossible to give every detail of the situation, story, <u>experience</u> or event. Time is too short. We have to leave some details out. Sometimes this is conscious, other times not. Sometimes the omissions are unimportant, sometimes they are vital.

SIX STEP REFRAME

A technique used for <u>strategy installation</u>, in which the individual 'seeks permission' from the internal self to make the change. The six steps are:

1. identify the problem
2. identify the secondary gain
3. ask the responsible brain to confirm
4. ask the creative brain for other ways of getting the secondary gain
5. check this is ok with the responsible brain
6. install

1. what's the problem (my clumsiness)
2. how does this help in some way (develops reflexes)
3. what other ways are there to protect the gain (eg learn to juggle)
4. does this work for me without me having to be clumsy? (yes)
5. how will you do this (get balls, instructions, practice) – will this work? (Yes).
6. do it..

The technique assumes there are two parts to the brain, that have to be checked out: the responsible (logical) brain (left hemisphere), and the creative brain (right hemisphere). The responsible brain makes 'sound' and rational decisions, but isn't great at creative solutions. The creative brain is great at generating new ideas, but not particularly responsible, being happy with risk. So both need to be 'on board' to create an innovative and appropriate solution. (See also <u>strategy installation</u>, <u>secondary gain</u> and <u>reframe</u>)

SLIGHT OF MOUTH (SOM)

A set of approaches designed to challenge strongly held but unhelpful beliefs.

See examples below

SoM: challenging the generalisation

Often by <u>exaggeration</u>.

no-one likes you? the whole world? every day?

SoM: changing the focus of the person

From a negative frame to a positive frame.

it's not about what you can't do, but about what you can do

see it less as a threat, more as an opportunity (see also <u>reframe</u>)

SoM: change the meaning of the belief

Getting a new <u>meaning</u> from the same behaviour – ie getting the other person to accept/believe something else.

when X, then Y...could also mean when X, then Z?

when he offers feedback that you find critical, could it mean not that he dislikes you, but that he cares enough to let you know how he feels?

SoM: identify the statement as only a belief

Challenge their view as only a belief – an invention, a construct, one option among many: a <u>choice</u>**.**

> so this belief of yours, which is only a belief, a point of view among many...

> your belief is a choice; you could choose to believe something else...

SoM: use the belief on itself

Challenge the way the belief works on and for the individual – especially if it is a limiting belief.

> how does that belief help?
> does that belief make you feel bad?
> how does that belief work for you?

SQUASH TECHNIQUE

Integrating two parts of self or other that appear to be in conflict.

> resolving internal tensions by finding common ground or purpose

The technique, simply described, is as follows:
- hold both your hands out in front of you palms up
- mentally, put one of the opposing ideas or positions in one hand
- put the other opposing idea in your other hand
- start to bring the two hands together, slowly....
- as you do, feel how you might 'work out' the contradictions and conflict; what is going to bring the two hands together in a way that will work?
- only clasp your hands together when you have a solution – either one idea will overcome the other, or you will find a 'third way' that manages to reconcile the two opposing ideas

I was working with an NLP Practitioner student (Charlie), who was writing a diary, and finding it beneficial. As part of his course work, he was also required to complete a weekly log. He was finding it difficult to do both, and chopping and changing between the two. It was only when he used the squash technique that he found his 'obvious' solution, of using his diary as his log....

STACKING ANCHORS

Use more than one anchor so they reinforce each other.

> For example a visual image, which has sound
> accompaniment, and an associated sense of taste or smell

I often have stacked anchors that combine visual and auditory – for example, key pieces of music are often associated with key events or places that I can instantly picture....

STATE MANAGEMENT

Managing your own, or someone else's, internal state.

Moving from
a negative to a positive state
the past to present
fully <u>conscious</u> to <u>trance</u>

<u>NLP</u> places a lot of store on an individual's internal state – how they feel and think; the <u>beliefs</u> they have, the emotions they respond to. Crucial is the idea that anyone's internal state is not a given, but a <u>choice</u> – and that it therefore can be owned, and amended, by that individual. So we each have the opportunity to choose our own internal state and, as coach, have the opportunity to help the other person manage their state, by moving from one which is unhelpful to one which is more helpful. (See also <u>calibration</u> and <u>inoculation</u>)

STRATEGY

The way, route, method or <u>process</u> chosen by the individual to do or achieve something. The way of getting from A to B. The 'how' of life.

> how the individual chooses to study or learn
> how an individual talks to someone else to persuade them to do something
> how an individual attempts to be happy

Strategy is an important concept within <u>NLP</u>. A key principle of NLP is that if there is a failure, it is a failure of strategy, rather than of the individual – it's not the individual that's broken, it's the strategy. So there's usually nothing wrong that a change of strategy wouldn't fix. This is so helpful, in that it separates the individual and the strategy, and the coach can work with the individual on the 'out there' (external) strategy, rather than the 'in here' (internal) person. It's not the person that has to change: it's the strategy. For most people, this seems more achievable, less threatening.

Everyone has and uses strategies to get things done. Often these are unconscious, and therefore difficult to change. It may be part of a coach's role to reveal the strategy currently being used unhelpfully (<u>strategy elicitation</u>) and work with the other person to create and use a more helpful strategy (<u>strategy installation</u>)

The key process (strategy) used by the coach is the use of narrative enquiry – 'what happened next' or 'how did that happen'. The emphasis is to discover the strategy, the sequence or flow of events, rather than interrogate for reason or motivation (why). Often the motive is unclear, or unhelpful, and asking too many 'why' questions can make the other person defensive. So the coach's role is discover the other person's story so that, at each point in the story, the coach can discuss with the other person whether there is an opportunity to intervene, and do something different at any point – ie change the strategy.

Asking someone to describe the event or experience also is less threatening for the other person, so they relax more, so the conversation is easier. This is particularly true for children and teenagers.....

I was working with Janet, who was having an awful time with her teenage daughter. Both would shout at each other a lot, and end up in tears. I used the narrative enquiry approach to find out 'what happened...and then what...and then what...' We then looked at each action (external) on the storyboard, and Janet's reaction (internal), and considered if Janet could change either the external action and/or her internal reaction if the situation arose again. Janet identified several points where a different action or reaction might work better, and agreed to try this. I met Janet a month later, and she was full of smiles. Her relationship was much, much better with her daughter, and she believed it was mainly down to the changes she had made to her strategy....

STRATEGY ELICITATION

Finding out how someone does things; how the other person works through a situation – discovering their method or process**.**

> so...how did it start...?
> ...and then what happened...?
> ...and then what....?
> and how did you feel about that...?
> and then what...?

This method is central to the Meta Model, and to drilling down.

The aim of strategy elicitation is to find out how the other person (or yourself) currently works through a situation, to get from A to B. This can be a mental or physical process, or both, and can be conscious or unconscious. The elicitation process essentially consists of the coach getting the other person to describe what happens, and how it happens (not why it happens). The process is something I call 'narrative enquiry' – finding out the way in which a person does something.

There are many examples elsewhere in this book where a change of strategy has really helped the individual (see for instance the stories provided under Ecology, Inoculation, Linguistics and Rep System). I have found it one of the most useful tools in my NLP toolbox.

Strategy elicitation is not just about discovering unhelpful strategies. A key starting point for Bandler and Grinder in formulating NLP was their detailed observation of people who they felt were excellent in what they did. So strategy elicitation is really helpful for understanding how really able people do what they do, so that we all have the potential to adopt that strategy, and <u>model</u> excellence.

I was attending an international NLP conference, and was sat with a group of people from across Europe, discussing teaching strategies in primary school. One colleague, from Finland described how in his maths classes, he had taught the narrative enquiry to his pupils. He then had recently observed the following. One of his pupils – Stefan – was clearly struggling to get the sums right. Two girls working on the same table, observed what Stefan was doing, and after a short while, went over to Stefan and said words to this effect: "Stefan, we've watched you, and we think you are using a strategy that explains why you get the sums wrong. Can we show you our strategy, and see if it's something you'd like to try...?" And they were 9 years old!!

STRATEGY INSTALLATION

Creating a new or amended strategy which is more helpful to the other person.

> where are you now?
> where do you want to be?
> what do you need to get there?
> what's stopping you?
> what action do you next need to take?

The above example is a 5-step model for installing a strategy (new or otherwise), where the answers are provided by the individual who wants to change, or simply achieve a particular outcome. The first two steps can be reversed – ie it may sometimes be more helpful to start with the aim, ambition or goal. (See also future pacing and TOTE)

S

STRUCTURE

In __NLP__ terms, this refers to the level at which information is accessed, processed and stored. A distinction is made between __deep structure__ and __surface structure__. Deep structure is the whole of our __experience__, retained in a combination of our __conscious__ and __unconscious__ self. Surface structure is the layer at which we are conscious of what we know and have experienced

> deep structure: everything you have read and absorbed in reading/accessing this book

> surface structure: what you can consciously recall from reading/accessing this book

A lot of our everyday __programmes__, which are really helpful to us, are given over to our deep structure – or unconscious self (walking, talking, driving, reading, even breathing) – we have no everyday 'conscious' awareness of doing these things, or of needing to remind ourselves to do them, or how to do them. This of course, frees us up to concentrate on the things that we do need to be conscious of – where we need to pay attention.

Examples such as those given above – reading and breathing, etc – clearly are helpful to us, being 'automatic', part of our learned but unconscious deep structure. But other unconscious memories and programmes may not be so helpful – and because we are unconscious of them, they may be difficult to 'consciously' access, retrieve and amend....hence the power of __trance__ and __hypnosis__, in accessing these deeper structures. (see the story about Sue given under '__deletions__') (See also __generalisations__, __distortions__ and the __Meta Model__)

SUBCONSCIOUS

See 'unconscious'

SUB MODALITIES

Sub-sets of the 5 modalities (VAKOG) used to change intensity.

for visual – bright/dark; near/far; framed/unframed; still/moving
for auditory – loud/quiet; multiple sources/single source; soft/hard; level/pulsing

Sub-modalities are most often used by the coach to help the other person access then modify their sense of an <u>experience</u> – eg in <u>visualisation, trance, fast phobia</u> cure or <u>swish techniques</u>.

SURFACE STRUCTURE

A shorter, less authentic version of the deep structure, and consisting of deletions, distortions and generalisations.

> so in response to the question: "how are you?" – if the answer is: "I'm fine"

In the above example the response is at the surface level – it contains no detailed information. The person speaking is bound to be making <u>conscious</u> or <u>unconscious distortions,</u> <u>deletions</u> or <u>generalisations,</u> potentially leading the other person to engaging in <u>mind reading</u> and <u>making assumptions</u> – which may or not be true.

SWISH PATTERN

Changing an individual's state from negative to positive, by changing the picture and/or its submodalities.

> picturing two images, one negative, one positive, then 'swishing' the negative one away, and replacing it with the positive image

One useful image for this is to use windscreen wipers. As the wipers move from one side to the other, they 'swish' away the negative image; as the wipers move back, they bring with them the new, better, more positive image.

If you wish, instead of changing the whole image, you can change the submodalities within the image...for example, for the negative image you could shrink the picture, make it fuzzy and out of focus, and move it into the far distance. It could have a negative audio soundtrack. The positive image would be the same, other than for changes in the submodalities – the image this time would be bright, colourful, sharp, near, and possibly moving. It could have a happy, humorous soundtrack...

Using swish can create trance or hypnosis, or be installed effectively once the other person is in trance or hypnosis. Swish is an example of creating an altered state.

S

SWITCHING REFERENCE

Changing the language's subject focus – in any of these combinations: first person (I); second person (you); or third person (they, it, the trainer).

> as I found, so you will find...
> "I was talking about.... and you will have noticed..."

The purpose of this technique is for the coach primarily to disarm the other person. By initially distancing the comment or story from the listener by using the first or third person reference, and then subtly making it about the listener, by using the second person reference.

As you read through this glossary, you will perhaps notice there are several times I have switched reference, from third person:
> *The coach will.....*

To the second person:
> *And you too....*

Or from first person:
> *On one occasion I was working with....*

To the second person:
> *Have you had that experience?*

S

SYNTACTIC AMBIGUITY

See 'ambiguity: syntactic'

SYNESTHESIA

The process of overlap between the 5 primary senses.

> as I see...I feel...
> on hearing...I feel...

If the coach does not yet know if the other person has <u>rep system</u> preferences, it can be useful to use this technique to ensure the listener is getting access to the full <u>VAKOG</u>. The coach should then <u>calibrate,</u> to notice any buy in or rejection signals in response to a particular <u>modality</u>.

TAG MARKING

Using the voice to mark the requirement/intention; downward tends to deliver a command or instruction; upwards tends to seek a response (question). (see also <u>analogue</u> and <u>digital marking</u>).

Da de $_{da}$. (down; command)

Da de ^{da}? (up; question)

Many people have a habit, or <u>programme</u>, of speaking with a particular inflection, or tone, without realising or intending it, or its consequences. So someone regularly using a falling tone may create an autocratic impression, without ever intending it. Similarly, someone with a habitual rising tone or inflection might seem uncertain or hesitant...

Of course, such tonal variations can also be used deliberately, to create an <u>altered state</u> in others, to create changes in mood and behaviour, just by varying the voice....

One tag I often use, conversationally, is 'make sense'. I can say it either with a falling tone – and use it to deliver an instruction – ie 'make sense of what I am saying', or I can use a rising inflection, implying a question, to check understanding = ie 'does this make sense to you?'

t

TAG QUESTIONS

A leading question, inviting agreement.

> this is easy, isn't it?
> that works, doesn't it?

Most often associated with the <u>Milton Model.</u> The coach is clearly asking the other person a question, which is always associated with a postitive ('easy', 'works'). So <u>subconsciously</u> the listener hears the positive word, and the invitation to agree with it

t

TEMPORAL PREDICATES

Words that refer to time and its passage.

> when..then...
> let's start with...
> now and then...
> sooner or later....

Associated with the <u>Milton Model</u>. These everyday phrases (and therefore non-threatening) attract little attention at the <u>conscious</u> level, but are useful in creating a clear sense of timing and expectation in the listener. So in the above examples, 'when... then...' is an example of a '<u>cause – effect</u>' statement, which can also be useful in <u>trance</u>:

> "when you close your eyes and relax, then you will feel..."

"Sooner or later" is in fact a <u>double bind</u>:

> "Sooner or later, the solution will come to you"

The only negotiable is time – ie when. Either way (sooner, or later) the solution will appear....

t

TEST FOR ACQUIRED

A process whereby the individual, after identifying a potential solution, is asked to run it in their mind, to check whether or not it is in place, and can work.

> "so, run your preferred approach through in your mind, checking out what happens, in sequence, and the effect it is having..."

This is the coach's way of getting the other person to validate their new <u>strategy</u> – to simply 'check it out'. A coach should also observe the other person as they do this, to <u>calibrate</u> any changes the new <u>strategy</u> might be producing in the individual – revealed for example, through a change in facial expression or body language. Generally speaking, if the test for acquired is successful, the individual running the test will look relaxed and calm, and possibly smile at the improved situation. (see also <u>future pacing</u>)

t

THE MORE....THE MORE....

**A specific form of <u>presupposition</u>, where two separate
elements are linked tied together.**

> the more you work at...the more you will become...

This is very similar to the 'when – then' example given earlier (see
<u>temporal predicates</u> above). Whereas 'when...then' is a temporal
(time) example, 'the more...the more' is a <u>cause-effect</u> example

t

THROUGH TIME

Where time is seen as a horizontal line in front of the individual, running from past/left to future/right.

> Past to the left, present straight in front, future to the right

This is one of the two classic <u>timelines</u> (see also <u>in time</u>). This option is often useful if the coach or the other person wants to look at their time line in a <u>disassociated</u> way: using through time, the individual's whole life is in front of them, almost as a display board, running left to right...

For some, the impact of being disassociated is less personal, less dramatic. It is perhaps less easy to separate the past from the future – since (visually) both are in front of the individual. It may be harder for the individual to put the past 'behind' them...

t

TIMELINES

A representation of time visually, as a continuum. There are two timelines: <u>through time</u> (left to right, in front of the individual); or <u>in time</u> (running from behind the individual to in front of them, and passing through them).

picture a time in the past...and now...and in the future...

Using through time, the individual is <u>disassociated</u>; using in time; the individual is <u>associated</u>. Other than that, there is no real 'difference' between an 'in time' view and a 'through time' view – both are equally valid. From the coach's point of view, however, it is important not to impose their own timeline preference on that of the other person, so the coach should check first how they 'see' time.

TOTE

Test, operate, test, exit; a modifying behaviour loop, designed to change unhelpful strategies.

> elicit the current <u>strategy</u>, then work out an alternative; then test, operate; test again (based on feedback); exit when the new strategy is in place and works

'Test-Operate-Test' is the loop, which continues until completed, when there is a need to Exit. So in devising, then trialling a new strategy, it is unlikely to work first time; there will be tweaks and refinements necessary. So in effect, the TOTE model might, in the real world, work something like this:

Design – operate – review – modify – test– review – modify – test – review – approve – exit

And the above is summarised in a simpler form as TOTE. (See also <u>future pacing</u>, <u>strategy installation</u>, <u>test for acquired</u> and <u>well formed outcome</u>)

t

TRANCE

An altered state of consciousness, moving the individual from a fully conscious state to a less conscious state.

so people can more easily access unconscious resources – the deeper structure

Trance can be self-induced, or be induced by a coach; trance can be accidentally or deliberately created. There are techniques to help create trance, but trance can also happen through an (accidental) combination of circumstances. So a coach could use hypnotic induction to create a trance; but equally an individual could enter a self-induced trance state by gazing into a fire... Perhaps less obviously, telling a story or metaphor creates a trance state – as you will know if you've ever watched a compelling film.... (see also fast phobia cure, hypnosis, induction and visualisation)

t

TRANSDERIVATIONAL SEARCH

Looking for <u>meanings</u> which might not be apparent in the surface <u>structure</u>, by probing that <u>surface structure</u> for deeper structure information and meaning.

> Can we go back to the incident you were describing...and look at it in more detail...?
> I'm curious to know more about....

(See also <u>Meta Model</u> and <u>drilling down</u>)

t

TRUISM

Statement of fact, which is non-contentious, obvious – to which the listener will unconsciously and obviously say 'yes'.

we're here today...
you arrived today...
you/we are sitting here...
today we are working on...

Associated with the <u>Milton Model</u>. The use of truisms has the benefit of creating two states: agreeing, and agreeable.

An agreeing state is created because the truism is a non-contentious fact – a statement of the obvious. Since the other person can only agree, then a pattern is developed of listener agreement – of the other person agreeing with what the coach is saying. So already, informally and <u>unconsciously</u>, the coach is creating an <u>altered state</u> of agreement, of consensus.

Secondly it is more pleasant to agree. It is agreeable to agree. So the coach is also, through truisms, <u>inducing</u> an agreeable state – one which is pleasant, comfortable, relaxing...one in which the other person is more likely to be open and receptive.

UNCONSCIOUS

That part of self which is present within each individual, but hidden from, and usually unknown to, that individual.

> meanings, feelings, thoughts, beliefs, emotions
> and behaviours

All the above examples can exist at the <u>conscious</u> or unconscious level. Many people are consciously unaware of, for example, how they breathe, or walk, or fold their arms. Many habits are unconscious – we are completely unaware of doing them or how we do them.

Most of these unconscious behaviours are harmless, or even helpful: if we had to consciously think about everything we do or need to do (like breathe, walk, talk), we'd be exhausted...! Being able to put a lot of our everyday thoughts, skills, processes and actions on 'the back burner' frees us up to focus consciously on the things we need to concentrate on.

Sometimes we can discover parts of our unconscious self by accident. Something will trigger a memory you had 'forgotten' – didn't know you had. Someone will mention something you do, that you had no idea you were doing (clicking a pen, playing with a piece of jewellery, biting your lower lip when agitated....). But... it's only possible to change any of these factors once we become conscious of them. Imagine I asked you to change an irritating behaviour you have, but that you are unconscious of...what would you do? Clearly, you'd need to know what it is before you can action it.

This is why all those elements that are part of our unconscious –

often summarised as our 'unconscious self' - are so important: they have a major impact on our lives, but (by being unconscious) are out of our (conscious) control. We cannot consciously control what we are unconscious of. In one sense, our conscious self is victim to, and governed by, our unconscious self.

So if our unconscious self is having an unhelpful impact on us, we would probably want to change it – but can't....unless we can identify what it is.

With practice, effort and key techniques, parts of the individual's unconscious self can be accessed, and be brought to the conscious level. And, once there and known, can be examined and if necessary, changed.

One of the aims of NLP is to make ourselves and others more aware of our unconscious self, and as a result, gain a better understanding of how and why we feel, think and behave as we do – and, where appropriate, make changes. (see also hypnosis and trance)

A friend of mine, Stella, was unaware that she always referred to her elder daughter as 'bright', and her younger daughter as 'lively'. This only became 'known' to her through a casual conversation. Stella was horrified, in that she was accidentally – unconsciously – stereotyping her two children in different ways, something she never intended. It was only with the realisation that she was doing this that she was able to change her behaviour, and the way she described her two children.

Consider the following scenario:
A man takes his son out for a drive in his car. They are involved in a car crash. The father is killed outright and the son is badly injured. He is rushed to hospital. The surgeon comes into the operating theatre, takes one look at the boy and says, 'I can't operate on that boy - he's my son.'
Do you find the above a puzzle, or is the answer immediately apparent to you? For those of you unsure of the answer, it is given at Appendix B at the end of this book – along with the relevance of this scenario to the unconscious self.

UNIVERSAL MODELLING PROCESSES

The filtering mechanisms of <u>deletion</u>, <u>distortion</u> and <u>generalisation</u>.

leaving information out, exaggerating, stereotyping....

Every individual has to filter information, in order to make sense of it, give it <u>meaning</u>. We simply cannot absorb everything – at a <u>conscious</u> level. So every individual (universal) has to reduce all that is in the world around them to some set of meanings. So everyone models the world – ie creates versions (or maps) of their world, which can never fully represent reality – but simply be some form of model of it. The processes we each use to do that typically include deletions, distortions and generalisations.

Can you picture the London Underground map?

It is perhaps the most iconic map in the UK. It is instantly recognisable, and works brilliantly as a guide for visitors. In fact, it is so powerful, that many people's map of London is that provided by London Underground. However, this map is not an accurate representation of where the stations are, to scale, or in accurate geographical/spatial relationship to each other. Nor does it represent the different depths of each tube line – it is 2D, rather than 3D. So often a visitor will change tube lines to get from A to B, when in fact, it would have been quicker to walk from A to B on the surface. The London Underground Map filters the complex reality of 'London' through (deliberate) deletions, distortions and generalisations, to create a model (or map) that works well – perhaps better? – than the 'real' world it represents....

UNIVERSAL QUANTIFIER

Statement given as if true for everybody or everything.

> nobody loves me (nobody?)
> I'm always rubbish at.... (always?)
> I could never please my father (never?)

A sub set of <u>generalisations</u>, which in turn is part of the <u>Meta Model</u>.

UNSPECIFIED VERB

The verb is too generalised, leaving the detailed <u>meaning</u> open to interpretation.

> "I want to improve"
> "I want to change"

A sub set of <u>generalisations</u>, which in turn is part of the <u>Meta Model</u>.

In the above examples, the verbs are 'to improve' and 'to change'. But what , more specifically, does this mean? Improve – in what? How? Why? Change – what? How? Why? Unless these questions are asked by the coach, there is a danger that the coach and the other person will give different <u>meanings</u> to the unspecified verb.

UNSPECIFIED REFERENTIAL INDEX

See 'lack of referential index'

VAKOG

The 5 <u>modalities</u> by which we receive (and filter) information.

<u>Visual, Auditory, Kinaesthetic, Olfactory, Gustatory</u>

Together the 5 modalities are known as the <u>Representation or Rep System</u>. All the information that is 'out there', in the world, is filtered and shaped by our combination of these 5 senses – it is how we make sense of the world.

Each person's 'mix' of these 5 senses is unique. Some of us will be very strong visually, but perhaps have a poorer sense of smell (olefactory). Someone else may not be strong visually, but acutely aware of sounds (auditory). It is partly this unique 'mix' of VAKOG that creates each person's map of the world. Understanding that we each have different maps due to this may help us appreciate the different viewpoints and perspectives that others have to what appears to be the 'same' <u>experience</u>....

A coach may often attempt to <u>calibrate</u> the other person's VAKOG preferences, so that they can match their approach to those preferences, helping to create better understanding and <u>rapport</u>. Similarly, if you were wanting to influence or persuade someone to do something, you might have more success if you worked in the other person's preferred <u>modalities</u>, rather than your own.

In life, of course, the way information is presented to us is not tailored or matched to our modality preferences: so it might be worth working to develop strengths in all 5 modalities, so that we are not disadvantaged in our access to information.
Each individual's VAKOG preferences in effect can represent their learning style or strategy. Some people access and retain

information better if it is in a visual form, for example. One school I know deliberately ensures that its pupils are exposed regularly to all 5 modalities, so that each pupil develops strengths across the VAKOG range.

In presenting my information on my Practitioner programme, I provide text based workbooks (with visuals) – but also 40 or so audio files of about 10 minutes, each dealing with one or more key NLP principles or techniques. Some who struggle reading through the workbooks, find the audio files a real help; for others, the reverse is the case.

Finally, I worked for a local authority which produced a booklet explaining the Council's financial regulations. On the left hand page was a full explanation, in text. On the right hand page was a flow chart representing the same information in diagrammatic form. Personally, I was drawn to the visual first, which then helped me understand the text. But what most impressed me was that the author had provided me with a choice....

VISUALISATION

The process of working through a current of future <u>strategy</u> by getting the individual to see the process in their mind.

> Select a time from your past when you were relaxed; can you recall such a time? Can you picture it?....

This technique is often associated with <u>hypnosis</u> or <u>trance</u> – though its success tends to depend on how visual the other person is.

Essentially the technique consists of encouraging the other person to visualise a sequence of events – either remembered from their past, or projected for their future. The coach leads the other person through the sequencing, by asking key questions. The other person typically remains silent, simply nodding, or clarifying where necessary. If successful, the other person enters a trance state, becoming immersed in the visualisation, and disconnecting from their actual real world, as their remembered or projected world becomes more real, and thus provides a powerful opportunity for greater recall (<u>strategy elicitation</u>) and potential change (<u>strategy installation</u>).

Although this technique is called 'visualisation', it may also make use of the other <u>modalities</u>: the coach might ask how something feels, how heavy it is (<u>kinaesthetic</u>); if there are any associated sounds (<u>auditory</u>); or if there is a particular taste or smell (<u>gustatory</u> or <u>olefactory</u>).

To demonstrate this process I asked my Practitioner group if anyone would volunteer, to address a particular concern they had. I reassured them that they would not have to say what their issue was. Karen volunteered. Karen was an excellent volunteer, and was *easily able to represent her issue visually and kinaesthetically, and work through a series of strategies for identifying, removing and obliterating her blockage. Throughout the process, though I knew in detail what devices and metaphors she was using (including an alien, a rubbish bin and a fire), I had no idea what her actual issue was, or what 'blockage' or obstacle she was working on removing and destroying. After 45 minutes she said the problem had 'gone', been destroyed. Having <u>tested for acquired</u>, I ended the session. Several weeks later I received an email from Karen. She said that she had been trying for 4 years to have a baby, without success. The issue she had been working on was the worry this was now causing, which she believed was contributing to the problem. That was the issue she had been working on with me in her visualisation session. She was writing to me now, to say she was, at last, pregnant. This may of course, have simply been a coincidence...*

VISUALLY CONSTRUCTED

Part of eye accessing cues, it is the assumption that someone looking up and to their right is picturing something in or about their future.

Visually imagining what it will be like to be retired, what they want to do on their next birthday, their 10 year old daughter's graduation

If these calibrations are correct, they can give the coach useful information about how the other person is processing information and thoughts. For example, in response to an initial question 'what issue do you want to talk about?', how the other person moves their eyes before answering can give the coach an idea if the other person is visualising, in which case they are comfortable with the modality, so the coach can use visuals and visual language with some confidence. It will also suggest whether the person's issue located in the past or the future....

VISUALLY REMEMBERED

Part of <u>eye accessing cues,</u> it is the assumption that someone looking up and to their left is picturing something from the past.

Visually recalling their school uniform; their first holiday, their earliest memory

(see comments immediately above)

VOCAL TECHNIQUES

Using voice to create change and maintain states

Slow, fast, louder, softer, emphatic at different points, rhythmic cadences; rich and powerful words

(See also <u>tag marking</u> and <u>analogue</u> and <u>digital</u> marking)

WELL FORMED OUTCOMES

End results for the individual which are positive, within their control, realistic, and fit in with the individual's <u>ecology</u>

> any goal, ambition or purpose the individual wants – job, personal change, be happier...

A useful mnemonic for remembering the four key ingredients for a well formed outcome (WFO) is PURE:

P: Positive – the objective is a positive statement, rather than a negative one

U: Under my control – the individual has ownership of whatever it takes to achieve – including personal commitment, and key resources

R: Realistic (or matched to the individual's <u>Rep System</u>) – the individual can see it, hear it, feel it, taste it, smell it....for real

E: Ecologically sound – this particular goal, and the way of achieving it, is compatible with the rest of that individual's world, priorities, life style etc – ie it doesn't produce conflicting or unwanted consequences

I was working with a group of three managers, who wanted me to help them organise and deliver a regional residential conference. They were very unclear about their outcomes. Using the WFO strategy I was able to help them set clear outcomes, and organise the sessions that were necessary to deliver these outcomes. One such outcome was for the participants 'to have fun'. I probed them on what this meant.

It was clear that 'to have fun' was positive (as opposed to the negative version – 'to avoid being dull and boring'); it was the other three parts of PURE that were challenging: could the organisers 'own' whether it was fun for the participants or not; what would each participant consider to be 'fun' in terms of their own Rep System? And how would this element support, and fit in with, the serious side of the conference? Having these elements in my mind (but not shared with the organisers) meant that we came up with a solution that met all four elements of PURE: the outcome was presented in a positive form (P); participants could choose whether to take part in the fun element or not (U); the fun solution was matched to what was known of the participants' preferences (visuals and auditory – ie music and colour in this case) (R); and to be focused on the end of the day, after the 'serious' stuff had finished (E).

X = Y

See complex equivalence

y

Z.

eye accessing cues

As seen from
<u>INSIDE THEIR HEAD</u>:

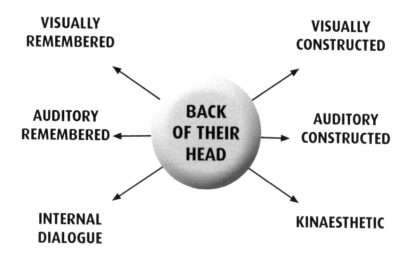

VISUALLY REMEMBERED		VISUALLY CONSTRUCTED
AUDITORY REMEMBERED	BACK OF THEIR HEAD	AUDITORY CONSTRUCTED
INTERNAL DIALOGUE		KINAESTHETIC

eye accessing cues

As you are
<u>FACING THEM:</u>

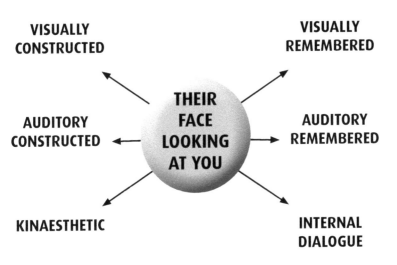

VISUALLY
CONSTRUCTED

VISUALLY
REMEMBERED

THEIR
FACE
LOOKING
AT YOU

AUDITORY
CONSTRUCTED

AUDITORY
REMEMBERED

KINAESTHETIC

INTERNAL
DIALOGUE

The father and son scenario:

> The surgeon is his mother.

If you did not get this as your answer, it is probably because your unconscious self maintains the belief that surgeons are men.

Your conscious self almost certainly knows that women can be, and are, surgeons. But if that is obviously the case, why did you not find that as your solution?

At the conscious level, most of us would want to believe we are not prejudiced.....

...but your unconscious self has led you to believe something different.

Which one – the conscious or unconscious self – won out??

APPENDIX C - NLP: A TABULAR GUIDE TO KEY TERMS

NLP TERM	SIMPLE EXPLANATION	EXAMPLE
Ambiguity: 1 phonological	Two or more words that sound the same but have different meanings	Here, hear; no, know; wait, weight
Ambiguity: 2 scope	Where it is unclear whether the descriptive word applies the word it precedes only, or everything that follows	Red table and chair Great golf and tennis player
Ambiguity: 3 syntactic	Where the word ahead of the noun is either an adjective or verb – it works either way	Milking cows Drinking water
Ambiguity: 4 punctuation	Creating two phrases joined by a phonological word	Glad to see you all hear what I'm saying
Analogue marking	Using the voice to mark the command; downward tends to lock; upwards tends to get a response. In units, fixed, as opposed to sliding (see digital marking)	Da de da. (down) Da de da? (up)
Anchor	Trigger or stimulus that (deliberately or unintentionally) prompts a particular response	Word, gesture, change of pace, sound, touch; place or setting eg a tune, smell, voice or photograph can trigger a feeling or memory – good or bad
Artfully vague	Using words and phrases in a vague, general way that allows and encourages the other person to fill in the detail that suits them. As such, it avoids contamination.	NLP is an excellent communication tool... You will find the resources you need...(also an embedded command)

Association	Being in the action, rather than watching self in the action	Go back to a time when you were cross with your sister; picture it; now.... are you there with your sister, feeling how you feel...in the moment, in the picture...
Assumption	A view or interpretation of the world that is not evidenced by pure and unequivocal facts; a perception as much to do with the person's interpretation of the event than the facts of the event itself	I assume you don't like me because you haven't phoned or didn't sit next to me in the refectory; I assume you are clever because you went to a 'posh' school....
Auditory	One of the 5 senses in the representational system (VAKOG), to do with sound	How people speak, the tone and volume; rhythm and tempo; music and other sound stimuli; awareness of background 'noise'
Auditory constructed	Part of the eye accessing cues vocabulary; if the other person's eyes are looking to their right, neither up nor down, they are often hearing something in the future	Hearing the crying of their as yet unborn baby; hearing the wedding bells of their approaching marriage
Auditory remembered	Part of the eye accessing cues vocabulary; if the other person's eyes are looking to their left, neither up nor down, they are often hearing something from their past	Hearing the school bell, and the dread it produced; hearing the squeal of brakes as they recall the crash they were involved in

Belief	A fundamental (and often subconscious) value, idea, or view of the world that typically influences or drives that person's thoughts, emotions and behaviours	Belief in a God, or fate, or luck; low or high belief in self; that 'life's not fair', or 'life is what you make of it'
Blowout (exaggeration)	Exaggerating something they habitually do/need so they become averse to it	Eating cream cakes; avoiding making initial contact in social settings
Brain	The part of the body where mental activity takes place. The hardware that allows the mind (the software) to do its work. Can be divided into different parts, each of which controls a different aspect of individual emotion and behaviour	What's inside the skull
Breaking state	See 'programme interrupt'	
Calibration	Assessing an individual's typical set of behaviours, appearance, demeanour and language, and noting any change in these which may provide insight into a particular trigger or possible internal state change in the individual	Change in colour (flushing, blushing, going white); change in behaviour (fidgeting, looking away or down); change in tone and pace of language (going quiet, speeding up)
Causal modelling (also known as linkage)	Words that imply a cause-effect relationship	You are like this, so you can... You do this, and you will also do...

Cause-effect	One thing causes another thing	As you relax, you will discover that... Because you have all you need, you will then work out.. Because you are studying X you will find that Y...
Choice	The freedom to make a positive and empowering decision from two or more options	Preferring to do A rather than B
Chunking	Taking the starting point, and creating new 'chunks' of information associated with that starting point, in order to create greater clarity or insight.	Up (Milton Model) making vaguer Down (Meta Model) – eg challenging distortion Across – creating an associated analogy
Circle of excellence	A technique to anchor a positive state by 'stepping into' the (imaginary) circle	Imagine a circle on the floor; visualise it; load it with positive energy; now, step into it and feel....
Comparative deletion	Missing standard of evaluation; lack of comparison: a statement of scale which lacks comparison	My children are not very bright (compared with...?)
Complex equivalence	One thing means the same as the other thing	X = Y - eg stereotyping – "he's an American, so..."
Conjunctions	Using connecting words such as 'and', 'before', 'while', 'as'...the purpose is to state a truism and link it to what you want them to consider, or to the state you want them to create for themselves	We will be sitting here and have a really good time... While you sit here you will find out...
Context	The setting or environment in which the event or situation takes place	Home, work, the past, the present.

Conscious	Known; mentally aware, and can be recalled and identified	A lot of the external world, and a lot of the person's internal state and experience (but not all)
Conversational commands (conversational postulates)	Asking a question that is heard as a command, so gain the response wanted without issuing a direct instruction	Can you describe your situation? Can you explain how you feel?
Deep structure	The full linguistic representation held by the individual you are trying to help or communicate with – ie what is restored when you get rid of deletions, distortions and generalisations	Everything from the individual's experience that is in either part of the conscious or unconscious self, and, to that extent, capable of the possibility of being accessed. This includes forgotten memories and events
Deletion	Leaving information out (consciously or subconsciously); not taking account of the 'full' picture	Choosing to ignore evidence that does not fit with my beliefs; being absent minded or over-focused
Digital marking	Sliding/variable scale of marking (as opposed to fixed – see analogue marking)	Eg slider switches or knobs on audio or lighting deck.. (can turn it up or down...)
Disassociation (or dissociation)	The person watching themselves in the action, rather than being in the action	Choose an event from your past (or future); can you see yourself in that event, as if you were watching a film of yourself, from a seat in the cinema...?

Distortion	Misinterpretation of information or misrepresentation	Putting a spin on information, either accidentally or intentionally; presenting a partial or biased picture
Double binds	Giving the individual a choice from two (or more) options, each of which will lead to the same (required/desired) end result	Concentrate by sitting or standing You can work on your own or in pairs Shall we meet before or after lunch? Do you want to tidy your room before or after tea?
Drilling down	Probing for further details, especially when the other person is offering deletions, distortions or generalisations	Always? All the time? Can you think of a time when this wasn't true? Can you think of another reason why he might not have phoned you?
Ecology	Extent to which any chosen action is acceptable to, or in synch with, the rest of the individual's values, needs or drivers	Taking more ownership does not put the individual under undue pressure or harm valued relationships; committing to extra study does not conflict with having enough time for family life
Embedded commands	Think of the suggestion you want to make, and wrap/package it into a sentence	As you let yourself go, you.. When you relax and... As soon as you finish your dinner you...You will find the solution as you... It seems as though you can start by...
Embedded questions	Where the command is embedded in a question rather than a statement	How would you see a way forward? How would you put a plan together for this?

Experience	Everything that impacts upon the individual – the life he or she has lived. The facts of that individual's life – everything that has happened to that individual, and which cannot be changed	You are reading this statement. That is now part of your experience – just like it has been your experience to read many hundreds of thousands of words during your lifetime so far. Every day of your life is your experience. These things have happened; they are facts; they are absolute; they cannot be changed
Eye accessing cues	Ways in which an individual's eye movements can reveal thinking patterns	See diagram at end of this glossary (See Appendix A)
Fast phobia cure	Way of getting someone with a phobia to re-experience a phobia-creating experience mentally, from a safe place, using a disassociation technique, leading to removal of that phobia	Fear of a particular animal (eg spider, rat, snake); fear of being with others; fear of flying
Filters	The various 'frames' we use, subconsciously, to see the world	Memory, VAKOG, RAS
Fractionation	Starting one story, then breaking off into another story, and perhaps another, before eventually completing them all	So there's this old man... who had a brother...who had a bike...now this bike....and this brother lived in Glasgow - have you been to Glasgow - no? well, you should, because....anyway...this brother...

Fragmentation	As coach, sounding hesitant, and failing to complete a sentence, as if struggling to recall information.... and so encouraging the listener to complete the sentence/find the information themselves	"So, the point I'm making is...that....er...." "So that's called...oh, what's the word...."
Future pacing	Asking the other person to check whether an idea or solution will work in the future, by checking it against their Rep System, before they do it for real	Look ahead and see yourself..imagine yourself having...how does that look, how does that sound, how does that feel?
Generalisation	Coming to conclusions about other situations from a single situation	Everybody.... You always....
Godiva chocolate pattern	A technique to encourage the other person to associate with a positive experience from their present/past, and thus be more open or receptive to a new idea or solution	Where is your favourite place? So, imagine you are there... what do most enjoy doing to relax? OK, so imagine you are doing this...right now....
Gustatory	Referring to the sense of a physical taste in the mouth	Sweet, sour, acidic, citrus, sickly...
Hypnosis	An altered state, a form of trance, which can either be self induced or induced by the coach, and can be accidental or deliberate, and in which the person becomes less and less aware of their conscious state and surroundings	Daydreaming, fantasising, drifting off', watching a movie, listening to a story

Indirectness	Leaving things vague, unspecified, so that the other person fills in the detail for themselves	Telling a story or offering a quotation that the listener makes relevant for themselves
Induction	Methods for creating a trance or hypnotic state	Gazing into a flame Watching a film Reading a book
Inoculation	Creating a context and state for the other person (or group) so they are less likely to have unhelpful expectations and feelings	Some might have an idea that...but most people find that... Does that make sense? Before we begin...
Internal dialogue	A conversation the individual has with themselves, mentally	"I'm not going to do that – it won't work, and I'll look a fool..."
Internal representation	See 'Representational System'	The 5 ways we experience and make sense of the world
In time	Where time line is seen as a line which passes through the individual, from entering the back of the individual and exiting from their chest	Future ahead, past behind, living in the here and now
Kinaesthetic	Referring to the sense of internal or external feeling	Touching, holding, grabbing, stroking
Lack of referential index	Unidentified pronoun, so the 'owner' is unknown (ie not referred to)	It can't be helped; we're all the same; they're out to get me
Linguistic	Language and non-verbal communication systems through which neural representations (VAKOG) are coded, ordered and given meaning	What we say (and don't say), and how we say it: words and tone.

Linkage	See 'causal modelling'	And, so, as well as
Logical levels	Different categories of information, arranged in a hierarchy or concentric circles, and intended to help the individual identify the level (or levels) that have most significance for them. They are: 1 Spirituality/world view 2 Identity 3 Beliefs and values 4 Capability 5 Behaviour 6 Environment	Examples for each level could include: 1 Religion, mission in life 2 Sense of self 3 Right, wrong, moral code 4 Skills, abilities 5 Key actions, habits 6 Conditions, surroundings, setting, context
Lost performative	A statement of fact or value judgement which excludes or omits the source of the assertion	Girls develop faster, intellectually, than boys; school children today just cannot concentrate
Matching (or mirroring)	Creating and sustaining rapport through being more 'in line/in sync' with the other person	Body posture, tone and pace of voice
Meaning	The interpretation given to any event or experience	The dog barking is being aggressive The dog barking is being friendly
Metamirror	Taking each of 4 positions (perspectives) in order to see things differently	Self, other person, observer, both of us/all

Meta model	The process of probing the other person's statements, to drill down for more detail. Often associated with tackling and challenging deletions, distortions and generalisations.	Who says? How do you know? Always, never, every? What do you mean by that? Compared to what, who? Who, what, where, when, how? Specifically...? What stops you? What would happen if you could? How do you know when you do that? Hang on, I'm not sure I'm with you, can you explain..?
Metaphor	Stories or incidents that convey the message you want to give, without it directly applying to the other person – so they make the connection for themselves	Fairy tales; Aesop's fables; 'Who Moved My Cheese?'
Metaphors -homomorphic	Generalised application	A story about feeling happy or positive...
Metaphors - isomorphic	Specific to an individual listener	A story about someone having an aversion to frogs...
Metaprogram	A 'big picture' framework or model of the world (maps) which shapes how we think	Towards/away from Proactive/reactive Big picture/detail

Milton Model	A set of processes and tools associated with Milton Erikson, to create conditions and statements which are artfully vague, imprecise and indirect, so that the other person has to fill in the detail themselves, and thus make the detail (and experience) relevant to their own world	Truisms, quotations, vagueness, metaphors, trance
Mind	The software within the brain	Feelings, thoughts, beliefs - the results of brain processing (neurology)
Mind reading	Making assumptions about the other person as if they were true..	You are probably thinking about... I expect you are now curious You might be feeling curious and slightly unsettled, and that is ....
Modalities	The 5 basic senses: visual, auditory, kinaesthetic, olefactory, gustatory (VAKOG). Our 'sense' of the world comes through these..	What we see, hear, touch, smell, taste...
Modal operators - Of necessity - Of possibility	Words that imply some level of commitment	Necessity: should, must, need, want, can, ought Possibility: might, could, yet, now, perhaps
Modelling	Finding someone who's excellent, and observing closely what they do and how they do it	Watching how Billy Connolly does what he does so well

Negative commands	Giving a command in a negative context – they cannot think of a negative without first thinking of the positive – 'don't imagine a blue elephant'	Don't think deeply about what you are learning.. You don't have to accept everything I am saying... It isn't necessary to work everything out... You don't have to be clear.. It isn't necessary to start feeling relaxed, open and confident

Nested loop	A more sophisticated form of fractionation, in which the speaker starts a series of stories, say in sequence A, B, C, D, and completes them in reverse order – D, C, B, A – so that each story is 'nested' or embedded within the other ones	A diagram can help here
		
		A A
		  B B
		    C C
		      D D

Neuro	Nervous system in the brain through which experience is received and processed through the individual's unique combination of the 5 senses (Rep System/ VAKOG)	How we access, interpret, process, store and retrieve information
NLP	Neuro Linguistic Programming: the relationship between how we interpret the world, how we communicate about and within the world, and how we develop predictable habits that shape how we function in the world	The feelings, thoughts we have, and the way we process them (neuro); the language and words and tone we use (linguistic); the habits we have (programming)

NLP presuppositions	A set of assumptions about the world and how we are within it, that underpin a lot of the ideas within NLP – ie 'where NLP is coming from'	Eg the map is not the territory; the meaning of the communication is the response you get
Nominalisations	Turning a verb into a noun, making the description more impersonal, and open to interpretation	There is a lack of communication
Olefactory	The sense of smell	Scents, perfume, fresh grass
Pacing	Moving into synch, in step, in tune, with the other person	Matching someone's speed of verbal delivery or walking pace
Pattern interrupt	A technique used to break the other person's habit, programme or state, before helping them replace it with another more helpful habit, programme or state	Sudden noise Interruption with a metaphor or story Taking a break Asking an unrelated question
Perception	The way each each person, sees and filters 'their world'	What do the following mean? Fire Flush Mobile
Positions (perceptual positions)	Different positions you can take to look at the same situation	First – self Second – theirs Third – independent onlooker Fourth - shared
Post-hypnotic suggestions	Suggestions made by the coach to the other person when the latter is in a hypnotic state	As you sit there, relaxed, you will begin to see...

Predicates	Process words like verbs, adverbs and adjectives which give us a sense of their preferred representational system	Sounds like, looks, like, noisily, colourfully....
Presuppositions	Assumptions about the other person or the world we take to be true	What commitment will you make to... How will you create an action plan... (also ec) How will you be more successful...(also ec) I know some of you will be... Once you are able to... What it will then mean is...
Presuppositions – adjectives/ adverbs	Designed to suggest a helpful and positive process or state	How easily, how quickly,
Presuppositions – awareness	Designed to raise consciousness – often an embedded command	Realise, become aware, notice, learn, discover, know
Presuppositions – change of time	Designed to place the thought (or embedded command) in a time frame	Begin, end, stop, start, continue
Presuppositions - commentary	Designed to create, emphasise or reinforce positives	Fortunately, happily, luckily, obviously
Presuppositions – 'or'	Designed to emphasise choice (implying that there is one)	Will you X OR Y?
Presuppositions – ordinal numbers	Designed to create a suggestion of sequence	First, second, last
Presuppositions – subordinate clauses of time	Designed to create anticipation, and sometimes to alter state	Before, during, after, while

Presuppositions of NLP (see NLP presuppositions)		
Process	The method or approach someone uses; the how, rather than the what	Eg how you learn, as well as what you learn
Programming	Behaving in predictable, subconscious ways; habit	Folding arms; sitting in the same place every time; reacting in the same way to the same triggers or stimuli
Quotes	Putting your intentions for them into someone else's words – so it is more removed, less consciously directive	Milton once said "you are all you need" My son once said: "you've got to practice to get anywhere" Gary Palmer said: "the harder you practice the luckier you get" Richard Bandler said: "man is a meaning making machine"
Rapport	Creating and sustaining empathy with another person	Congruent use of spoken and body language
RAS (reticular activating system)	The brain's filtration system that selects crucial messages from all the information that's available	3 key criteria are survival, novelty and emotional content
Reality violation (selectional restriction violations)	Giving a concept life, or giving a person an inanimate quality – creating something that cannot be 'real'.	This chair is sad Your confidence will carry you through... Your happiness will be your friend, and create new possibilities....

Reframing	Representing one view – usually negative – in a more positive way	Glass half empty, or glass half full problem focused, or solution focused "It didn't work" or "I didn't work at it"
Represent-ational systems	The five senses through which we experience the world	Visual Auditory Kinaesthetic Olefactory Gustatory
Resources	Set of nine personal assets we all have, or can develop, to help us in our life	Open, aware, curious, responsible, flexible, creative, fun, perseverance, pragmatic
Rules	A set of metaprogrammes, they are the expectations and boundaries individuals set that regulate that individual's judgement and responses	Things are either right or wrong, black or white; live and let live; take every opportunity and risk
Secondary gain	The benefit gained by the individual having the problem	Clumsiness produces quick reflexes; being a victim produces a rescuer and avoidance of responsibility
Self fulfilling prophesy	Associated with beliefs, in that having a belief makes the belief more likely to happen	Believing you have no confidence makes it more likely you will behave with no/low confidence
Self limiting beliefs	What the individual unhelpfully believes about themselves and the world often restricts or limits their actions and outcomes	I depend on others for my happiness I can't remember names

Simple deletion	Statement with missing or deficient information	Abraham Lincoln died at a theatre Mohammed Ali was a conscientious objector
Six step reframe	A technique used for strategy installation, in which the individual 'seeks permission' from the internal self to make the change	1 what's the problem (my clumsiness) 2 how does this help in some way (develops reflexes) 3 what other ways are there to protect the gain (eg juggling) 4 does this work for me without me having to be clumsy? (yes) 5 how will you do this (get balls, instructions, practice) – will this work? (Yes).
Slight of mouth (SoM)	A set of approaches designed to challenge strongly held but unhelpful beliefs	See examples below
SoM: challenging the generalisation	Eg exaggeration	Everyone dislikes you? The whole world? Every day, every second?
SoM: change the focus of the person	From a negative frame to a positive frame	It's not about, it's about...
SoM: change the meaning of the belief	Getting a new meaning from the same behaviour – ie getting them to accept/believe something else	When X, then Y...could also mean when X, then Z

SoM: identify the statement as only a belief	Challenge it as only a belief – an invention, a construct, one option among many: a choice	So this belief of yours, which is only a belief, a point of view among many... Your belief is a choice: you could choose to believe something else...
SoM: use the belief on itself	Challenge the way the belief works on and for the individual – especially if it is a limiting belief	How does that belief help? Does that belief make you feel bad? How does that belief work for you?
Squash technique	Integrating two parts of self or other that appear to be in conflict	Resolving internal tensions by finding common ground or purpose
Stacking anchors	Use more than one anchor so they reinforce each other	Eg a visual image, which has sound accompaniment, and an associated sense of taste or smell
State management	Managing your own, or someone else's, internal state	Moving from a negative to a positive state; the past to present; fully conscious to trance
Strategy	The way, route, method or process chosen by the individual to do or achieve something. The way of getting from A to B. The 'how' of life	How the individual chooses to study or learn How and individual talks to someone else to persuade them to do something How an individual attempts to be happy
Strategy elicitation	Finding out how someone does things; how the other person works through a situation – discovering their method or process	So...how did it start...?... and then what happened...? ...and then what....? And how did you feel about that...? And then what...?

Strategy installation	Creating a new or amended strategy which is more helpful to the other person	Where are you now? Where do you want to be? What do you need to get there? What's stopping you? What action do you next need to take?
Structure	In NLP terms, this refers to the level at which information is accessed, processed and stored. A distinction is made between deep structure and surface structure. Deep structure is the whole of our experience, retained in a combination of our conscious and subconscious self. Surface structure is the layer at which we are conscious of what we know and have experienced	Deep structure: everything you have read and absorbed in reading/accessing this book Surface structure: what you can consciously recall from reading/accessing this book
Subconscious	See 'unconscious'	
Submodalities	Sub-sets of the 5 modalities (VAKOG) used to change intensity	For visual – bright/dark; near/far; framed/unframed; still/moving for auditory – loud/quiet; multiple sources/single source; soft/hard; level/pulsing
Surface structure	A shorter, less authentic version of the deep structure, and consisting of deletions, distortions and generalisations	So in response to the question: "how are you?" – if the answer is: "I'm fine" – it is a response that is surface, not deep

Swish pattern	Changing my state from negative to positive, by changing the picture and/or its submodalities	Picturing two images, one negative, one positive, then ' 'swishing' the negative one away, and replacing it with the positive image
Switching reference	Starting with 'I', then switching to 'you'	As I found, so you will find...
Synesthesia	The process of overlap between the 5 primary senses	"As I see...I feel..." or "On hearing...I feel..."
Tag marking	Questions at the end, lock or invite a response	Won't you? Didn't you? Can't you?
Tag questions	Milton model: a leading question, inviting agreement	This is easy, isn't it? That works, doesn't it?
Temporal predicates	Words that refer to time and its passage	When..then... Let's start with... Now and then... Sooner or later..
Test for acquired	A process whereby the individual, after identifying a potential solution, is asked to run it in their mind, to check whether or not it installed, and can work	So, run your preferred approach through in your mind, checking out what happens, in sequence, and the effect it is having...
The more...the more	A specific form of presupposition, where two separate elements are linked or tied together	The more you work at...the more you will become...
Through time	Where time is seen as a horizontal line in front of the individual, running from past/left to future/ right	Past to the left, present straight in front, future to the right

Time line	A representation of time visually, as a continuum. There are two timelines: through time (left to right, in front of the individual); or in time (running from behind the individual to in front of them, and passing through them)	Picture a time in the past...and now...and in the future... 'in time' is associated; 'through time' is disassociated
TOTE	Test, operate, test, exit; a modifying behaviour loop, designed to change unhelpful strategies	Elicit the current strategy, then work out an alternative; then test, operate; test again (based on feedback); exit when the new strategy is in place and works
Trance	An altered state of consciousness	So people can more easily access unconscious resources – the deeper structure
Transderiva-tional search	Looking for meanings which might not be apparent in the surface structure, by probing that surface structure for deeper structure information and meaning	Can we go back to the incident you were describing...and look at it in more detail...? I'm curious to know more about....
Truisms	Statements of fact, non-contentious, obvious – to which the listener will unconsciously and obviously say 'yes' - Creating agreement - Creating agreeable state (state management)	We're here today... You arrived today... You/we are sitting here... Today we are working on..

Unconscious	That part of self which is present within each individual, but hidden from, and usually unknown to, that individual	Some meanings, feelings, thoughts, beliefs, emotions and behaviours
Universal modelling processes	The filtering mechanisms of deletion, distortion and generalisation	Leaving stuff out, exaggerating, stereotyping
Universal quantifiers	Statement given as if true for everybody or everything	Nobody loves me (nobody?) I'm always rubbish at.... (always?) I could never please my father (never?)
Unspecified verbs	The verb is too generalised, leaving the detailed meaning open to interpretation	"I want to improve" "I want to change"
Unspecified referential index	Used in NLP practice (part of Milton Model) to allow the listener to make their own sense of it	"You will notice a certain feeling" "This is helping"
VAKOG	The 5 modalities by which we receive (and filter) information	Visual, Auditory, Kinaesthetic, Olfactory, Gustatory
Visualisation	The process of working through a current of future strategy by visualising the process in the individual's mind	Select a time from your past when you were relaxed; can you recall such a time? Can you picture it?....
Visually constructed	Part of eye accessing cues, it is the assumption that someone looking up and to their right is picturing something in or about their future	Visually imagining what it will be like to be retired, what they want to do on their next birthday, their 10 year old daughter's graduation

Visually remembered	Part of eye accessing cues, it is the assumption that someone looking up and to their left is picturing something from the past	Visually recalling their school uniform; their first holiday, their earliest memory
Vocal techniques	Using voice to create change and maintain states	Slow, fast, louder, softer, emphatic at different points, rhythmic cadences; rich and powerful words
Well formed outcomes	End results for the individual which are positive, within their control, realistic, and fit in with the individual's ecology	Any goal, ambition or purpose the individual wants – job, personal change, be happier...
X equals y	Another term for complex equivalence	See complex equivalence

Term	Example
Ambiguity	'let him have it'
Ambiguity phonological	'rhodes'
Ambiguity syntactic	Shaving cream
Anchor	3 pieces of music; visuals
Artfully vague	Mind map
Assumption	Coffee
Auditory	Cafe
Beliefs	Wanting to do my job
Brain	Break in
Calibration	Arms behind head
Causal modelling	Memory
Chunking	Concrete sheep
Complex equivalence	Dating – no text
Context	Staying quiet at home
Comparative deletion	GCSE gaps
Deletions	Sue – disappointment
Digital marking	Stefi – controls
Disassociation	Skydiving
Distortion	Neville – drowning
Double bind	Accessing nlp (go to logs??)
Ecology	Learning preferences
Gustatory	Medicine, school dinners
Generalisations	Clumsiness I
Hypnosis	Baby in class
Indirectness	Museum
Induction	Ways of self-induction
Inoculation	No role play
Lack of referential index	'It didn't work' & clothes
Linguistics	Presentation to midwives
Logical levels	Relationship across levels
Lost performative	Elise – self deprecation
Meaning	Geraldine

Metamirror	Fagin
Metaphor	'Are You Sitting Comfortably?'
Metaprogram	Charles
Milton Model	Katie & Sandra
Mind reading	Cathy
Modal Operator of Possibility	Brian
Negative Commands	Clumsiness
Olfactory	Handkerchief
Pacing	Energy to reflection
Perception	Marking Andy's script
Predicates	My visual preferences
Presuppositions ....time	'Before we begin...'
Process	Multiplication rap
Programme interrupt	Worry to problem solving; my dad
Rapport	The knight and the dragon
Reframing	The journey; keeping fish
Representational System	Rachel's visual preference
Resources	Poem
Rules	Inflexibility
Secondary gain	Clumsiness II
Self limiting beliefs	4 minute mile; achievers
Squash technique	Charlie
Strategy	Janet and her daughter
Strategy elicitation	Finland
Switching reference	I...the coach....you
Tag marking	Make sense
Unconscious	2 daughters; father and son
Universal modelling processes	London Underground map
VAKOG	3 examples
Well formed outcomes	Residential

Book design by Jo Fenwick, Fenwick Design Consultancy Ltd
jo@fenwickdesign.net